# Shadow Work

CW01500032

## FOR THE

# Soul

# Searcher

*A ten-step guide to authentic
self-expression*

Polly Pollock

VERBENA

# Contents

# Welcome to Shadow Work

Firstly, welcome to your Shadow Work journey! As you sit and read the first page of this book, take a deep breath, relax your shoulders, and let it sink in that today you make the decision to become your most powerful, unique and badass self. As corny as it sounds, this is the moment that you decide to set yourself free, and that's exactly what Shadow Work allows you to do. By taking this journey, you release the boundaries you place upon yourself in everyday life, learn to feel more at home with who you are, and create things that you probably think right now aren't possible.

Shadow Work, I feel, doesn't get spoken about enough as a life-changing tool. We hear about the concept of it sometimes and we know the basis of it, but it's so much more than just a psychological theory or spiritual concept. Shadow Work is not only a way for us to connect more deeply with the hidden parts of ourselves, it's the start of a chain reaction that allows us to dream bigger, achieve more, change our reality and live authentically as who we really are. The inner work that we do spreads to our external lives like wildfire when you know how to harness your shadow, which is exactly what I'll be teaching you on this journey.

The chapters in this book will help you bridge the gap between you and your truest self. You may be thinking at this point one of two things, either: "Me and my truest self are worlds apart, I don't even know where to start" or "I'm already my true self". If you're thinking the first, by the end of this book, you'll see how close your truest self has always been, just waiting to be unlocked. If you're thinking the second, tell me, why did you pick up this book? We can often think we are living in our purpose or our true self for many reasons, such as validation from others, pressure from friends and

family, false positivity and more. I urge you to keep an open mind when reading this book to explore parts of yourself that may be vastly different from who you're living as right now.

I wrote this book with my former self at the heart of its creation. My former self was disconnected. She was self-critical, a slave to her own limits, hungry for freedom and authenticity, and honestly, utterly lost. If you can relate to these things in your present or past, then this book is for you. Only a few of us discover Shadow Work in a world that wants us to be a machine and not prioritise this type of inner work. The system, the patriarchy and Western societal norms don't want us to be freethinkers, which is why we don't get told about this type of personal work often.

That being said, things like therapy and spiritual development (that go perfectly together) are becoming very much the norm, which of course makes me a very happy camper! We are slowly blending this type of development into the everyday, and we have access to it more and more. We're at a pivotal point in time where we are taking our power back. I think that the most radical thing you can do in this life is to be true to yourself, no matter what your peers, society, your family or your uninspired bosses might say.

If I had a dollar for every time someone told me I was living in dreamland since I began my Shadow Work journey and ultimately started feeling deeply connected to myself, I'd be filthy rich. But guess what? (And this is the secret that we aren't supposed to know, yet seems stupidly obvious once you work it out.) There are no rules to how we live life. Apart from paying taxes and a few other bits here and there, we can do whatever we set out to do. However, here's the caveat: we have to start, and starting is often delayed by lack of self-belief, unresolved traumas and lack of confidence to act upon what we really want. All of these things are connected in a web that we enter when we go on our Shadow Work journey.

## WHO THIS JOURNEY IS FOR

You're probably reading this because you've reached a point in your life where you know you want to make a change of some kind. You may have decided it's time for you to repair the relationship with yourself so that you can feel happier and be more expressive, and more authentic to you, or maybe you want to delve into Shadow Work to give yourself the confidence to make a change in a specific area of your life.

This book, ultimately, is for anyone wanting to walk the path less trodden to explore what you can really make of your life, without needing to hide who you are.

## WHAT THIS JOURNEY IS AND ISN'T

So what's the catch? It's not a quick fix. As humans in the modern world, we love a quick fix, right? We long for someone to just give us the answers or a pill to make it all better, but these things don't come from you, do they? Shadow Work and healing is a sovereign journey, which means that it's up to you to work on it. At the end of the day, no one knows you better than yourself, and although it's not a quick fix, it does become easier when you start to surrender and listen to what your inner voice wants to tell you.

This journey is a practical, step-by-step process to understand yourself more and open yourself up to boundless possibilities. Shadow Work can often seem elusive and, honestly, a bit scary to many people (the name doesn't exactly sound like rainbows and butterflies, I know). The fear of the process and even the name comes down to the fear of working through difficult things, which we're not taught to do in life, so it can feel pretty foreign when we start doing it. In this book, I'll be demystifying the idea of Shadow Work to make it accessible and practical, blending it with some gentle spirituality.

Within these pages, you'll find tools that you can rinse and repeat going forward in every stage of your life. Shadow Work isn't a one-off process, although the first step is usually the most important and impactful. In order to reap the full benefits of this type of inner work, we need to keep an open mind throughout our lives so that we can recognise when we need to revisit our shadows. I still find myself going back over my own tools for Shadow Work when I get imposter syndrome coming in. Writing this book was one of those times!

## EIGHT KEY PRINCIPLES

Here are my eight key principles for this journey that I'd like you to refer back to when you feel that you need a bit of grounding or balance. Shadow Work can bring up a rollercoaster of emotions. Sometimes you're going to feel empowered and strong like you can take on the world, sometimes you're going to feel ungrounded, and sometimes you're going to feel hurt, but if there's one thing I can promise you, it's that feeling it all is 100 per cent necessary and 100 per cent worth it.

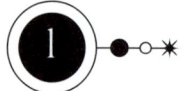

Your past does not define your present. It's a tool that you're using to better your future and you are in full control.

Perception is everything. This work is a luxury as well as a necessity. You can make it as fun, energising and transformational as you like.

You are completely ready to go on this journey. If you weren't, I promise you, you wouldn't have picked up this book.

 Remember to celebrate when realisations and breakthrough moments come up – this is going to be key to your expansion.

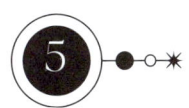 Feel it to heal it, but know your limits. When emotions come up, we absolutely need to feel them, but make sure you have your boundaries in place so that you're ready to take action again once you're ready.

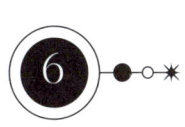 Positive self-talk seems so simple, yet so many of us struggle with it. Throughout this journey, be kind to yourself and watch the way you're talking to yourself. Catch yourself in the act if you end up saying something nasty to yourself, and reframe it into something kind.

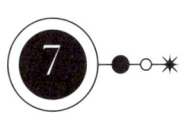 Nurture yourself and your Inner Child. Talk to yourself like you would talk to the child version of yourself. Have plenty of patience, compassion and love for yourself throughout this process.

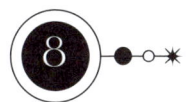 You've got this. You really have. If you've been made to feel weak or disconnected from your power in the past, here's where you take it back. This is your time.

## DIVING INTO SHADOW WORK

So, where does Shadow Work actually come from, and how has it expanded into what it is today? Let's go over a brief history.

Shadow Work was originally a concept created by Carl Jung, who was a 20th-century psychoanalyst. Although Shadow Work has come a long way since then, and has been developed as a more spiritual concept, it's important to recognise its roots.

In Jung's theory, we, as humans, often don't see that we are made up of multiple parts, including our shadow. The Shadow Self is made up of the parts that you keep hidden or suppressed due to them either being unpleasant to think about and deal with, or out of the fear of showing them to the world.

Jung believed that in order to be our most authentic selves, we need to first address and recognise those hidden aspects by confronting our shadows and digging deeper into why we have them. When we don't address these parts of ourselves, they can end up unconsciously controlling our lives.

Jung also mentions that the goal of Shadow Work isn't to bring awareness to it and then get rid of it, but to integrate it into our lives. In my view, the work then goes much deeper as we need to unpack certain feelings and fears around integrating and ultimately expressing who we are to the world.

**Jung also developed the theory of the four archetypes of the psyche:**

# 1  The Persona

Our persona is how we appear in the world, it's like the mask we wear to show to those around us. If you've ever heard of the term masking, this is very similar. Our persona isn't our truest self, it's what we choose to show to others depending on the situation we're in. To a degree, our mind will automatically do this as a survival mechanism, to allow us to be a functioning member of society. However, it can often take over, disconnecting us from our true selves.

# 2  The Anima/Animus

This is essentially what creates balance within us so that we can understand, relate to and co-exist with people who are opposite to us. It also helps us to understand who we are in more detail.

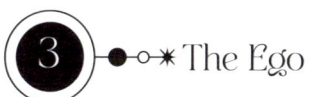

# 3  The Ego

The ego is related to the persona, however, the ego is about your sense of self and how you genuinely view yourself. The ego decides what you do in life, the choices you make, how you feel, and lives within the conscious part of your mind. Similarly to the persona, the ego is there to "protect" us, but it can get carried away and make us lose sight of the other parts of who we are and what we can achieve.

# 4  The Shadow

The shadow is the unconscious part of the self that holds our repressed traits, deepest desires and natural instincts. The shadow is the part of ourself that we usually deny in order to keep it from being seen.

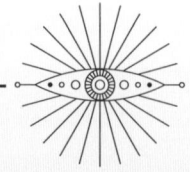

This book, ultimately, is for anyone wanting to walk the path less trodden, to explore what you can really make of your life, without needing to hide who you are.

## MY VIEW

Shadow Work has evolved alongside a changing world. Issues, traumas, limits and people have changed drastically since Jung's theory was first developed, so it makes sense that Shadow Work has also adapted. Over the years, Shadow Work has been accessed more in the self-help and spiritual space, giving people the chance to work through their individual issues in a more soul-led and self-led way.

Now that we've gone into the roots of where Shadow Work comes from, I'm going to give you my take on it and tell you a little more about how Shadow Work has developed and changed in the modern day.

In my experience of working within spiritual and personal development, there are a few main themes that come up more than any others:

- Self-worth and confidence

- Imposter syndrome around what is possible in this life/what you can do

- The fear of being seen as a spiritual, creative or magical person.

Personally, I think we're seeing these things come up more and more because of how quickly the world is changing and how our human consciousness is expanding. We're being more inquisitive and less regimented than ever before.

We're recognising that we now have the choice to go against the things that were once social norms, but no longer make sense for us in this world. This ultimately wakes us up to a lot of unconscious programming and shadows to work through, because when we try to break away from those things, we're met with a wall of fear around our personal growth.

Shadow Work in itself has also evolved from being very heavily focused on the mind to bringing in many other factors involving the body and the spirit. We're looking deeper than our actual life experiences to work out why we think and feel certain ways, for example, the witch wound and how it's now been scientifically proven that trauma can be passed down generation to generation (I'll be going into this a little more in Chapter 6).

# My Personal Story

My Shadow Work journey started at a pretty unexpected time in my life. I was working in a dead-end corporate job, questioning whether I was going to start my business up full time again, which, at the time, was spiritual counselling along with reiki and tarot reading. I remember sitting there thinking of all the ways that it couldn't work, all of the reasons why I should be staying quiet about my dreams, repeating all of the stories that I had been told by others my whole life. I honestly thought that I'd never be able to even start my own business let alone thrive in it whilst empowering others all across the globe.

I was in this headspace for a few months, unable to give myself a metaphorical kick up the arse to do something about it, so, the stars aligned and did it for me and I was made redundant.

"Your position isn't needed anymore, and we're going to have to let you go."

Crap. I'm screwed.

I remember thinking, for a moment, that my whole world was ending. How was I going to live? What was I going to do? I wasn't qualified enough to get another job like this, and I didn't want to work in a job where I was overqualified and bored. I was literally stuck.

My ex-boss then went on to tell me that they were giving me three months worth of pay, which ultimately paid for three months of me setting up my business! This, however, took a while to sink in. Even though I had just been handed an opportunity on a plate, after three or four months of planning ways I could start my business back up, I was still so scared and so certain that it couldn't be done.

Where was this rhetoric of "you can't do it" coming from? It was literally repeating itself over and over in my head like a broken record. Even in the first few months of working for myself, I was thinking "enjoy it while it lasts, you'll be back in a 9 to 5 before you know it". I now recognise that voice as my ego (I'll be discussing how to get to know and work with your ego throughout this journey, too).

Those first three months of me setting up my business was really when the Shadow Work consistently started, and I began to see all of the ways that old narratives and past experiences were affecting my life as a whole, not just in my work.

I was recognising so many things. I had been so disconnected from myself for years that I was basically asleep, just following someone else's orders and rules. I was blocking myself from happiness, confidence, opportunities, fun, money and love, just from that disconnection and distrust in myself.

# THE START OF THE JOURNEY

I remember the day I first sat down to get started on my first bit of Shadow Work. I had decided enough was enough and I was done with feeling like this. I was recording video diaries at the time, which I highly recommend for keeping track of your personal progress, as well as journaling. It was a New Moon in October, and I still re-watch it from time to time to remind myself how far I've come. I remember the first words I said on that video, which were, "I don't know, I just think I can do something better and I'm worth more than where I'm at right now".

On the video, I immediately started to cringe and followed up my statement with something along the lines of "oh no, that sounds really bad" or "that sounds so vain".

Because that's the hard part, isn't it? We're taught all our lives to not love ourselves too much or to just keep our heads down, so that when we do start addressing our shadows and making changes, we get hit with this strange feeling of guilt and shame just for feeling better!

From that point on, I started to go deeper by asking myself questions about why I felt a certain way about things, why I refused to compliment myself, why I refused to let myself properly feel my emotions or show vulnerability. Every opportunity that came up, I asked myself "why". I set aside time to dig deeper into those parts of myself, and showed myself compassion along the way, which is also an incredibly difficult task when we're also heavily programmed not to feel sorry for ourselves.

Showing compassion to yourself absolutely gets easier along the way, but it didn't start off easy for me. At the time, I didn't think that I actually deserved any compassion. After all, I was a corporate woman focusing on swimming with the big fish and getting paid more – I couldn't possibly let myself feel anything, so I told myself.

## MEETING THE EXPERIENCES

Within my Shadow Work, the main areas I knew I needed to focus on were self-worth, confidence, financial independence, my relationship and, well, my overall happiness.

If I were to pick one out of all of those that seemed to be the root of everything I had pulled up during the first stages of my Shadow Work, it would be self-worth or confidence. The more Shadow Work I did, the more past experiences I was able to get closure on that were all responsible for chipping away at my confidence over the years.

It's all well and good meeting with your shadow, but if we don't also meet with the experiences that caused the shadow in the first place, we can't get closure and find logic in why it's there in order to move on. The experiences I had to revisit were uncomfortable at times. I didn't want to think about the things that made me so emotional and upset because I never got closure on any of them when they happened. Most of them I didn't even validate at the time because, to me, they were just normal things I had to go through.

I remember working backwards through my Shadow Work journey, starting with the job I had just come out of and how the bosses in my last two or three jobs were all very good at manipulating me into believing that there was nothing for me unless it was in the corporate world. I was able to trace it all back to the first sales job I ever had when I was 17, and how I was always fed the same rhetoric of "you need a safe 9 to 5 job". This helped explain my scarcity mindset about how it's just not possible for a woman of my age and experience to start her own business. Oh how I laugh at that now!

Of course, there was a lot more to these realisations than I can fit in here – I'd fill the whole book up if I gave you the full story!

# FITTING THE PIECES TOGETHER

I started to trace my feelings and emotions back to the pattern of dependency that kept popping up in my past. I was always so reliant on others, usually those who had no interest in truly being there for me. I was able to recognise that I was so reliant on those types of people because I had no self-belief or self-worth. This was the very thing that got me into hanging out with the wrong people in my late teens and early twenties.

When I started doing my Shadow Work on these things, I recognised that I was drawn towards toxic people because I had such low self-worth, caused by other toxic people from my childhood. It was all starting to come together in my mind: how I had been hiding the unique and authentic parts of myself because that's all I'd ever known to do – it was like a survival mechanism for me.

I have always been a good judge of character, I know when people aren't good for me and always have, but I chose to surround myself with those people regardless because I felt like I couldn't do any better as a result of that low self-worth.

I traced it back even further to my younger years. As far back as I could remember, I was always bullied for being different and quirky. People just didn't like me, I made them uncomfortable. I realise now it's because I always wanted to shine my light, I always wanted to be myself, and people who are stuck in their ways trying to bring others down to their level don't like that, they resent it. I started to see how everything linked up, from my academic achievements and opportunities, to my body confidence and boundaries, or lack thereof.

This was where the work deepened for me and I started building from the ground up. The more I was able to bridge the gap between what I felt in everyday life and past experiences that were responsible for creating each shadow part of myself, the more I felt like I was able to let myself off the hook a little, and have some understanding for myself. It was a new feeling, that's for sure.

I was very aware at the time that, whilst these experiences weren't my fault, it was my responsibility, and solely my responsibility, to work through them to better my life and regain connection to who I was.

Now, don't get me wrong, these types of experiences aren't going to be easy to talk about for many of us. Getting closure and logic with something doesn't mean that the discomfort will just magically disappear, and it can still catch us out from time to time.

Shadow Work is a lifelong process, even years after you've crossed the first hurdle. You'll still, at times, get the ego coming in to trip you up, but it's how you deal with the intrusive thoughts that really matters. When you start becoming familiar with using Shadow Work in all areas of life, it will become much easier to recognise your patterns, go into why those things pop up, and tell them "thank you, but goodbye!" much more quickly.

Fast forward to what my story looks like now: I've done a heck of a lot of inner work, which didn't always feel easy, but it's what allowed me to understand my patterns, my past, my self-sabotage, my barriers and how to move past them. It's not only made me the happiest I've ever been, but it also allowed me to realise that my purpose is serving others. I'm now a published author, a mentor, a speaker, a visionary, and I'm doing things I never thought I'd be able to do.

Without my own Shadow Work, there's absolutely no way I would be doing the work I'm doing today, and I feel so grateful that I made the choice to do it.

I wonder what you'll discover your soul purpose to be after you've done your Shadow Work? Ultimately, I believe that our purpose is to be happy in our own skin, but our deeper purpose often comes out when we do the inner work to become ourselves.

As I said at the start of this book:

*The inner work that we do ends up spreading to our external lives like wildfire when we know how to harness our shadow.*

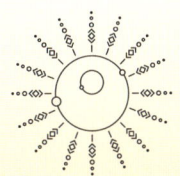

It was all starting to come together in my mind: how I had been hiding the unique and authentic parts of myself because that's all I'd ever known.

# CHAPTER 1

# Who Are You, Really?

When you're on the journey of self-rediscovery, it's a pretty big question to ask yourself: *who am I, really?*

So many of us live our lives being someone we're not, usually at the service of others. We get swept up in all sorts of identities that define who we are. When you meet someone new, one of the first things that usually comes up is "so, what do you do?" and we reply with our job role or what we spend our days doing.

"I'm a delivery driver" or "I'm a stay-at-home mum" are things that we instantly say in response to a question like that, but they don't actually say anything about us. We see this as our own identity and fill our days with those things, which in turn disconnects us even more from the question of who we are at our core.

In this first step on your Shadow Work journey, we're going to be focusing on three things:

- How you see yourself
- Identifying and accepting all parts of yourself
- How you mask yourself in the world.

## HOW YOU SEE YOURSELF

It's important to allow yourself to see beyond the surface. Whether you're young and just starting to discover who you are in the world, or older and trying to see beyond the years of having a certain identity, what I want you to focus on here is stripping all of the external away in order to see you as your most raw self.

We can often get caught up in the pressures of the modern day, and it can get dangerous when we allow that to be our whole self. There's the idea that we have to fit into a purpose all the way through our lives. In our 20s, it's the idea that we need to be buying property and being a part of hustle culture. In our 30s and 40s, we're expected to have children, raise a family, get promotions and get rich, and then in our 50s and 60s, there's the pressure to retire – and when you do, you feel like you've lost your purpose.

To really figure out who you are at your centre, you need to release, to a certain degree, the need to do something or be something by the standards of others, and remember this when you're in the process of discovering who you are. Your true purpose comes to light after you connect deeper to who you are and regain your true sense of self, rather than placing your value on external factors.

When you dig further into how you see yourself, I want you to remember that no feeling is bad or good right now. We're going to cover that further down the line. Right now, it's about being honest with how you see yourself in your life right now and meeting yourself where you're at.

Being self-aware isn't something that we are naturally taught in the modern world, which is why it can feel a little bit uncomfortable to start going into who you are and all of these deeper layers, but the more we do it, the easier it gets.

Your true
purpose comes
after you connect
deeper to who
you are and
regain your true
sense of self.

## IDENTIFYING AND ACCEPTING ALL PARTS OF YOURSELF

As we grow older, we tend to feel the pressure to "grow out" of things, to change who we are to fit a mould, to hide away parts of ourselves that once felt so magical. Yet, we also need to learn to love and accept those parts of ourselves that don't feel magical at all and make us feel scared.

Now, when I talk about loving and accepting all parts of yourself, I don't mean that you should recognise where you need to grow and "accept it" rather than putting the work in. What I mean by loving and accepting all parts of yourself is that there may be parts of you that don't "live up to" the unrealistic expectations of the world and yourself. There may be destructive and difficult parts of yourself that need working through. However, loving and accepting yourself in the place that you're at right now and meeting yourself where you are from a place of self-love and compassion is key and all part of integrating the Shadow Self.

Looking deeper into this, we bottle up a lot of resentment and anger because we hide authentic parts of ourselves, which makes us feel destructive. It's important that you allow yourself to explore with childlike curiosity during the Shadow Work process, and be open to seeing multiple parts of who you are.

When we think of self-love, more often than not, many of us think "I'll love myself when...", which just instils the message that we're not good enough as we are. True self-love begins when you learn to love yourself at your lowest point, when you bring awareness to the fact that you don't have to be perfect in order to love yourself and accept all parts of yourself.

So, starting now, I want you to drop all of the barriers and set out on the mission of loving yourself as the imperfect version of yourself, because the truth is, we will never be "perfect".

## HOW YOU MASK YOURSELF IN THE WORLD

Recognising how we show ourselves to the world is one of the most important parts of Shadow Work, as it allows us to go into the "why" behind it. As I mentioned earlier on, this is something our mind will naturally do to make sure that we're functioning members of society, but what we want to look at is when this turns into concealing who we are out of the fear of judgment.

It can be really tricky to bring these things to light as this conditioning really starts from a young age. We're taught not to stick our heads up above the parapet and that children should be seen and not heard. For many of us, we were told through multiple areas of life that in order to be respected and safe, we need to conform rather than be inquisitive and challenge the norm.

This is where the work begins with unpacking what you do in order to be accepted by others, and what actually comes from your own personal values, likes and dislikes.

Social conditioning is something that runs deep within us, usually deeper than our view of self, because we get used to seeing the majority of those around us act a certain way day in and day out. Ultimately, the reason we tend not to show that we're "different" is because we're worried we will be demonized for it.

We bottle up a
lot of resentment
and anger
because we hide
authentic parts
of ourselves.

## CONTINUING THE WORK

You may have had a specific area of your life that you wanted to focus on when you picked up this book, in which case, it may be a little bit easier to look at your current beliefs. However, if you're covering your life as a whole, I would recommend splitting this into a few different areas and revisiting them as and when you need to, for example, work and finances, relationships or self-worth. This will likely happen naturally on your Shadow Work journey anyway, as we constantly have new things coming up for us, but for the purposes of not overwhelming yourself, I would start with the area of your life that you feel needs most attention right now.

Throughout this work, the more vulnerable you can allow yourself to be, the better. Remember to see it almost like a deep-dive meeting with yourself, rather than a character assassination. Doing this part of your Shadow Work from a place of self-love and honesty allows you to be more open in recognising things that need to come out.

# Practical Exercise

We're now going to journal about what we've discussed in this chapter to expand on how you see yourself. The goal here is to create a domino effect by digging further into the layers of who you are when you revisit these prompts later.

If you're familiar with journaling, that's great! If this is your first time, then remember that there's no right or wrong way to go about it, and my only piece of advice is to allow yourself to have no filter and be patient with yourself. Digging into your subconscious is a work in progress, and the words don't always flow out easily to start off with.

If you go through these journal prompts and feel blocked or frustrated, just remember that you're only at the tip of the iceberg and this is only the first part of your Shadow Work journey. You've got a lot more to cover, and you'll be constantly revisiting your relationship with, and thoughts about, yourself, so don't overcook yourself on this.

Remember, if you need a boost, you can always head back to my Eight Key Principles at the start of the book.

1. How do you describe yourself and who you are without including your job roles, looks or hobbies?

2. How do you view yourself? What are your current opinions on all aspects of yourself?

3. How do you think others view you?

4. What parts of yourself do you hide or are you actively scared of other people seeing?

5. Are most of your daily actions based on other people or yourself?

6. What parts of yourself can you openly recognise as destructive/imperfect/negative?

7. What parts of yourself make you feel the emotion of shame?

8. What parts of yourself are you proud of, taking away all standards, opinions and expectations of others?

9. What are some of your traits, quirks and unique qualities that you used to have as a child, but have now been suppressed?

10. If you had a magic wand, what would you change about yourself?

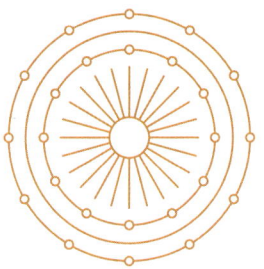

# CHAPTER 2

# Tracing It Back

Here's where your work really begins. Once you've become aware of what you currently think and feel about yourself, and you've started to pay attention to all parts of yourself, allow it to sink in and become comfortable with it. Just by bringing those things into your awareness, you have allowed yourself to be vulnerable with yourself so that you can grow.

When we start to study our shadows and trace where they come from, things start to make a lot more sense.

When I teach Shadow Work, I like to simplify it all by saying that we have two main layers of the Shadow Self to work with:

- Our blocks and limits in life

- Our repressed personality/true self.

Both of these layers interlink, and ultimately, both are likely caused by external factors, such as other people and environmental factors. I have mentored many women who have a fear of expressing who they really are and don't believe in their capabilities, both of which are caused by other people's opinions, expectations and judgment.

Ultimately, our core beliefs that we have in adult life start when we're young, so when we start to trace our beliefs back, we may start to see patterns of where it all started. Tracing our current beliefs back to their origin is non-negotiable when it comes to personal growth and Shadow Work, and although it may not be the easiest process, it allows us to put logic into what we feel in our day-to-day lives. Bringing logic into it is almost like a sigh of relief. Most of us will spend years barely touching the surface of why we act and feel certain ways – we mostly just end up feeling bad about who we are because of those feelings and thoughts.

## GETTING COMFORTABLE WITH THE UNCOMFORTABLE

What we're doing here is recognising actions and thoughts, looking at how they make you feel, and then doing the work to trace it all back to the origin. You'll almost certainly be carrying this on long after you finish this book, as we usually see more and more realisations come through about our origins and why we are the way we are. Shadow Work, in general, gets easier the more you put in, but it can be like opening Pandora's box – there can be some tough realisations and it can be very emotional to work through them.

No one really likes venturing out of their comfort zone when they do it the first couple of times. But the comfort zone is never actually comfortable, is it? Otherwise we wouldn't be trying to venture out of it. The comfort zone is really just our zone of familiarity, it's where the ego in our mind likes to pitch a tent and camp out, which is why the ego is the first thing to pop up to warn us of the "dangers" when we start to explore.

So yes, whilst it can all be uncomfortable to start off with, the more you do it, the more you'll see that the discomfort of it all is a tiny inconvenience in comparison to what you get out of doing the work, although it may not seem like it when you start out.

# WORKING WITH TRIGGERS

When we start to trace these things back, we're likely to get triggered at some point – there's no two ways about it. A trigger is essentially when intense emotions such as hurt, sadness, panic or anger come up as a result of something we have usually heard, seen or witnessed, taking our mind back to a painful or traumatic time (sometimes subconsciously). Our triggers, whilst uncomfortable, come in to let us know that there's a deeper issue at play that still needs to be worked through, so ignoring your triggers is essentially like putting a lid on the whole process.

When you notice your triggers coming up, be inquisitive about them. Ask yourself the following questions:

- What is the feeling or trigger that is coming up (such as shame or fear)?

- What was the situation that caused the trigger (such as you were rejected from a job offer)?

- What is this trigger really about? What is this feeling taking you back to (such as the feeling of being told you wouldn't achieve anything as a child or young adult)?

- What is this trigger asking you to work through in the present day (such as feelings around self-worth and your ability to persevere even when presented with rejection)?

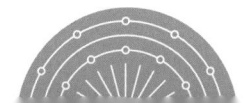

Adjusting your perception around triggers and what they mean for you can be a really useful tool to trace back where things are coming from in real time. It's very easy to see our triggers as a destructive thing, usually because we have this perception that our "negative emotions" are shameful and not okay.

I completely disagree with this, which is why I'm so passionate about holding space for others to feel their emotions. I'm a firm believer that you need to feel it to heal it, however, it's also about knowing how to channel those emotions and use them as a tool so that they don't become destructive for you.

This is where seeing your triggers as a tool rather than an inconvenience comes in. When you get into the habit of loving and accepting yourself and your triggers, you start to see that they're coming in for you to grow. The more you listen to them, learn from them and take action to move away from them, the easier it becomes.

If you feel like your triggers are unmanageable or if you feel unsafe at any point, I would recommend seeking help from a therapist or doctor you trust.

Your triggers do
not make you
weak, they allow
you to become
stronger and
more self-aware.

## LOOKING AT OUR ROOTS

When we start to trace our current situations back to their origin, it becomes clearer why we've ended up hiding who we really are. Ultimately, our feelings are linked to our actions, and if we feel like we need to change who we are in order to fit in with our environment, that could send us on a trajectory that isn't right for us in this life.

Our blocks that we're currently facing, whether it's feeling like we have no life direction, like we're disconnected from ourselves or generally feeling unhappy, all in some way link to repressing certain parts of us, which links back to our experiences.

All of this usually links back to other people. I've never worked with anyone who hasn't linked the root of their low self-value, blocks and beliefs to someone else when we go into it. As I said before, this all usually starts in childhood or young adulthood.

When I first got into my Shadow Work and I started tracing my low self-worth back, a question that popped up for me was, "Well, why would people say things if they weren't true?". I had gotten so used to taking everything that someone else said as gospel because I was never taught to trust myself, so in turn, I thought that it was all true. When you're not taught to empower yourself growing up by those around you, it almost certainly will play a part in your adult life.

Of course, the more you venture through adulthood, the more you learn how people work, why they do things, and often, how the most wounded people will be the first to shoot you down. This is what I started to see the more Shadow Work I did: people indoctrinate us with their opinions and beliefs and we take it as fact. People do this from a place of fear themselves, and you'll often find that the brighter you shine your light, it acts as a beacon for both those who want to lift you up and those who want to shoot you down. You just have to get into the swing of having your own back to deal with those who aren't on your wavelength.

## UNMASKING

I want to look more closely at the concept of masking and how and why it's important to take off the mask when you're doing your Shadow Work.

When masking is all we've ever known out of the fear of judgment and the need to blend into our environment, it can be very tricky to separate yourself from that. For this next section, I want you to show up as your most raw and vulnerable self, and when you're journaling, just allow anything underlying to come through.

Dropping the mask is also about trusting yourself. I know it can feel daunting to start showing up as you, mainly because you may not be sure who that is right now. You may also feel scared that by dropping the mask and allowing yourself to be vulnerable, you'll be opening yourself up for people to shoot you down.

All of this is the animalistic instinct within us to survive, but it takes our own self-awareness to expand beyond that point and give ourselves the time and compassion to heal.

When we move onto the exercise at the end of this chapter and start tracing it all back, I want you to keep an open mind to revisiting all parts of your life. Of course, it's important to find the root of our beliefs, but it's also important to recognise the patterns, too. Some things may flow out easier than others, and sometimes the most transformative realisations are buried the deepest, so be patient with yourself as you unearth these things.

When I say patterns, I'm talking about the ongoing themes that you pick up on relating to your beliefs, blocks or underlying issues. Once we've identified our beliefs and where they come from, we can start to dig into the patterns that they have created for us.

## THE CYCLE

When I was younger, I used to drift towards toxic people by default and was in soul-sucking jobs that I hated. I had very low self-worth. I struggled to be alone and I had no trust in myself that I could ever do anything on my own or achieve anything in this life. I was always trying to be someone I wasn't and repressed all of my unique traits. When I started going into the "why" behind it, I realised that this low self-worth came from severe childhood bullying and lack of encouragement to use my discernment and empower myself, amongst other things. It wasn't until I dug into the issue of low self-worth and gained closure on the root cause of the issue that I was able to break away from the patterns and ultimately, the block.

So the cycle that kept me trapped can be summed up as:

- The Block: Being in soul-sucking jobs and feeling unhappy with life

- The Feeling: Low self-worth and self-trust

- The Root: Childhood bullying and no discernment

- The Pattern: Drifting towards toxic people and remaining stuck at The Block.

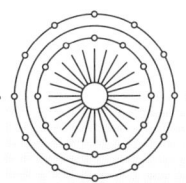

You just have to get into the swing of having your own back to deal with those who aren't on your wavelength.

Are you starting to see how all of this interlinks? By the end of this chapter, you'll hopefully be able to identify your blocks, your current beliefs, the root of those beliefs and the patterns they create in your life.

Of course, we'll be going into the specifics around how your true self has been repressed as a result of this, but for now, focus on these key points for the Practical Exercise.

In section one of the exercise, you'll be revisiting certain questions from Chapter 1 about your current beliefs, tracing them back to their origin and starting to unearth the patterns.

In section two of the exercise, you're going to summarise everything you've picked up on in section one. You'll be asked to summarise the main block you're actively struggling with and then create your own Cycle as I did in The Cycle so you can map things out and make the next part of your Shadow Work journey a lot more simple.

Remember, there's no set way to do this exercise, you can make your writing as long, short, clean or messy as you like, and you can even do it for multiple areas of life if you want to come and revisit it another time. But for now, I would recommend sticking with the main thing that comes up for you.

# Practical Exercise

**SECTION ONE: FINDING THE ROOT**

Revisit questions 2, 3, 4, 6, 7 and 10 from the Practical Exercise in Chapter 1 and for each question, ask yourself and write down the answers to the following questions:

- Where do those beliefs come from?

- Can you trace those things back and identify the first time they were instilled into you (who said it, where was it, when was it)?

- From these realisations, are there any patterns that you can pick up on that seem to play out in your life as a result of what you feel or believe about yourself?

**SECTION TWO: THE CYCLE**

Now fill in the following categories, given what you've learnt above, based on my example:

- What is the Block?

- What Feeling does it create?

- What is the Root of these feelings?

- What Pattern does it create?

Feel free to journal about any additional feelings, thoughts or realisations that have come up for you.

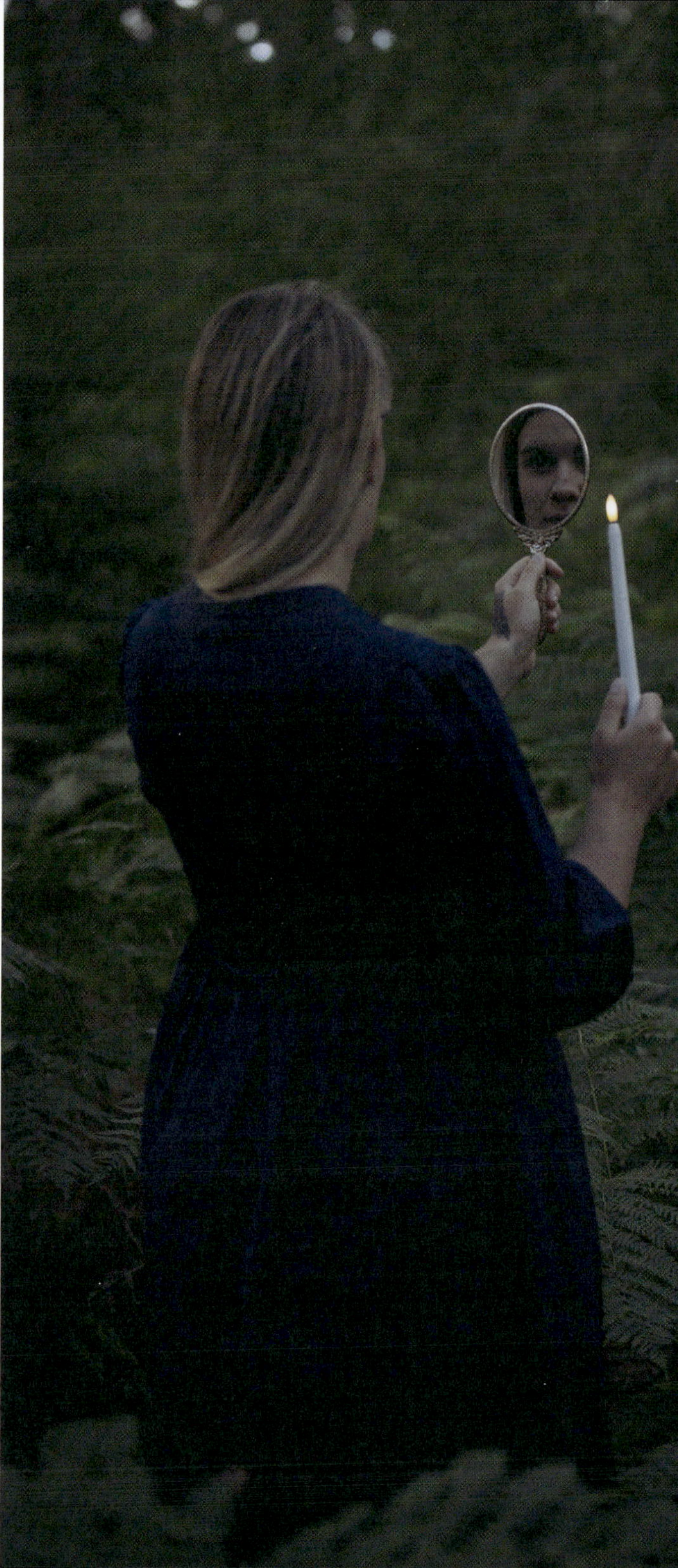

# CHAPTER 3

# Your Inner Child

Now that we've done some digging into your present and your past, I want to talk about Inner Child work.

Inner Child healing has become an incredibly broad topic and is often spoken about, which is fantastic. However, I often feel that the real bones of the work is overlooked, like many things in personal/spiritual development. In this chapter, we're going to be doing a deep dive into what makes this work so important and how you can use it in your Shadow Work.

Inner Child work, or Inner Child healing, is essentially the process of working out what parts of your current situation link back to childhood situations, emotions, upbringing, events and behaviours. However, a big part of this work that is usually overlooked is reparenting your Inner Child after figuring out those links.

Most of us will have parts of our Inner Child that were neglected in some form. Most of us grow up and realise that there were certain times when our needs weren't met, causing a disconnect in adulthood. This is where reparenting your Inner Child comes in.

Connecting, meeting and integrating your Inner Child is such a key part of Shadow Work. Without it, we are still neglecting that version of ourselves. Whilst Shadow Work is about integrating repressed parts of our personality and our traits, it's also about recognising that there are different past versions of ourselves that have an important role to play in our present.

45

## DISCONNECTING TOO SOON

So, why do we become disconnected from our Inner Child? It would be hard to pinpoint exactly when this happens because everyone's experiences are different, but ultimately, I believe that this happens when we feel forced to "grow up". Many of us feel that we have to grow up too quickly because of the pressures of the world, the pressures of other people and how you appear to the world. There could be many reasons as to why we disconnect from our Inner Child, but usually it's because we feel we have to do it to survive in the world, similar to why we repress parts of our personality.

I can remember even the smallest, minor details about me stepping away from my child self. I was watching everyone grow up around me, talking about the latest pop stars and fashionable clothes, whilst I still had my "head in the clouds", wanting to create magic, to go adventuring in the forest and find fairies – which is why barefoot nature walks make my Inner Child so happy and giddy in the summer!

I remember really struggling with the idea of letting the child version of me grow up, and when it happened I felt gutted, and in turn I grew up double the speed and never looked back, which was something I had to come to terms with when I did the Inner Child part of my Shadow Work.

Of course, there's an element of this that's needed. We ultimately do have to grow up and be adults, but when we completely disconnect from our Inner Child, things start to feel bleak, and we end up being confused as we don't align with what our heart wants.

Our Inner Child holds our heart's desires, our creativity, our playfulness, our fun – even our higher mind and intuition is connected to this version of ourselves. When we repress and ignore it, we get so caught up in what's expected of us, over-worrying and being susceptible to indoctrination. We become clones of everyone else rather than our own individual person.

For me, I knew that my Inner Child work was absolutely crucial to not only my own healing and growth, but to be able to serve others. There were so many natural, beautiful gifts and talents that I had repressed for so many years. The funny thing is those beautiful gifts and talents were hidden away because I thought that they made me "weird" and "different", like it was a bad thing. When we choose not to do this Inner Child work, we risk losing all of those incredible parts of ourselves.

When we do ignore our Inner Child (which most of us do for a very long time without knowing that's what we're doing), we essentially get stripped of our unique qualities and our unique magic. We also don't give ourselves the chance to process any of our experiences as a child, which can be detrimental to the choices we make and the experiences we have in adulthood.

Realistically, unless we instigate the work ourselves, we won't usually get the chance to do this work. We don't have the capacity or the self-awareness to process this stuff in childhood, and then before we know it, we're catapulted into adulthood and put on the hamster wheel of life, where we're told that nothing is wrong, so we don't question it until we have our own personal awakening.

It makes sense that it takes us so long to get around to this work, meaning that we have even more things to dig into as a result of ignoring our Inner Child (such as our patterns and current beliefs). However, it's better late than never, right?

# RECONNECTING

Reconnecting with your Inner Child and giving your younger self the love and validation that they deserve, whilst putting those fragments of who you really are back together, is truly one of the most rewarding parts of this entire journey.

Something that many people find difficult when reconnecting to the child version of themselves is having compassion. It can be especially difficult if you're someone who has the subconscious narratives that you're not worthy of that, or even a lack of safety when revisiting the child version of you.

Whilst it can be scary and uncomfortable sometimes to reconnect to these aspects of you, it's 100 per cent necessary and such an important part of rediscovering who you are. This version of you isn't some long lost memory, it is YOU, and you deserve to be heard, appreciated and loved. I truly believe that if we have things that our Inner Child wants us to address, it needs to be done by us, which is why Shadow Work overall is so important: nobody knows us better than we know ourselves.

So, when you do reconnect with your Inner Child, try and act with the love and compassion you would want your own child to feel. This mindset makes it a lot easier to be compassionate and patient with yourself in this process.

When you first begin to connect to your Inner Child, notice any emotions or feelings that come up whilst you're connecting. Note them down and go into where they could be coming from, and reinforce the feeling of safety that you have now. When things get a little difficult in Shadow Work, I suggest regrounding yourself by having a little mantra such as "even though this feels x, I love and accept this part of my journey, knowing that I am safe now to do this work". This really just helps to bring it all back into the present so that you can ultimately feel safe and secure.

For me, I knew that my Inner Child work was absolutely crucial to not only my own healing and growth, but to be able to serve others.

## A CRUCIAL AGE

So, when we look at the current beliefs and blocks that you discovered in Chapter 1, and you traced back in Chapter 2, how many of those are linked to something that came from a childhood, teenhood or even early adulthood experience? What we tend to find with beliefs that are heavily engrained within us is that they more than likely come from childhood or teenhood. Statistically, the majority of our core beliefs that we have in adulthood are formed between the ages of seven and nine, however, depending on your own personal experiences, it can vary.

I wonder if you can do some more digging, whilst you refer back to the beliefs and blocks in Chapter 1, into what you felt around the ages of seven, nine, or even older at perhaps 12 or 13? How can you start to dig into what your Inner Child feels about your current beliefs and where they come from? What are the feelings your Inner Child has toward the situation?

I'll use the same example as in Chapter 2 so that you can see how the cycle can often tie together:

- **The Block:** Being in soul-sucking jobs and feeling unhappy with life

- **The Feeling:** Low self-worth and self-trust

- **The Root:** Childhood bullying and no discernment

- **The Pattern:** Drifting towards toxic people, keeping me stuck at The Block

- **The Inner Child:** I feel like I have no friends, people think I'm weird and it's not safe to be who I want to be.

Go ahead and try this exercise as a continuation of Chapter 2 and try to connect with how your Inner Child really feels. It can be really useful to talk in the present tense and speak as the child version of you. Try to allow the initial words and phrases to come out, and if you feel yourself blocking it, try to backtrack and allow the words to come out as they need to.

## THE INNER CHILD

Listening to the feelings that come up from your Inner Child is the first step towards acknowledging and understanding where it all comes from. Try to allow the words to flow out as you write them, and don't worry if it's not as clean or summarised as the rest of the points; the main thing here is that you reconnect with the things associated with your Inner Child.

The feelings that your Inner Child may present to you might not always be the most comfortable, but they usually come up for a reason. A good way to think about it is sometimes children can appear to be acting irrationally. They have temper tantrums in the middle of a supermarket, or shout, hit and scream. Children do this because they are in the process of figuring it all out when it comes to experiencing all of the emotions that life hands them. It appears irrational to adults, because we know how to filter our emotions most of the time, however, the child is learning.

This is also happening with your Inner Child, especially if you're someone who didn't get the chance to express their emotions in a healthy way as a child, or were shamed for feeling and saying certain things. Our Inner Child shows up with "irrational" behaviours when we get triggered, scared or overwhelmed. Sometimes we have certain reactions and think "where did that come from?" A lot of the time, it comes from our Inner Child becoming frustrated because we're not listening to their needs. This is why the reparenting part of Inner Child work is so important. It's all well and good understanding your Inner Child, but without reparenting our Inner Child, we're just accepting it.

## REPARENTING

There are many things you can do to reparent your Inner Child. One of these is to have regular catch ups with your Inner Child. Ask them what they want to be heard about. These are worthwhile as, often, we have such a disconnect with our Inner Child that we need to rebuild those connections by stating things out loud or on paper. If you're a visual person, then guided meditation is something that works incredibly well, which is one of the things I do within my work with others when we do Inner Child work.

Another way to reparent is to ask yourself what used to light you up as a child? What did you used to love doing that you haven't been able to do in a while? Look at how you can make space to do those things. Let go of your worries around how you'll look or what people will think and prioritise having fun with your Inner Child by doing this exciting activity.

Make time each week, even if you're super busy and only have 20 minutes, to take yourself on an Inner Child break, feeling the peace and joy that it brings you. Add magic into the everyday where you can, buy more colourful sticky notes for your office, eat the food that your Inner Child enjoys once in a while, make time to not focus on logic, but real fun. When was the last time you had real fun? Fun that doesn't involve watching TV with a glass of wine or going out socialising in "adult" places. I set you to the task of making Inner Child time once a week and watch how the world becomes a little more colourful again, whilst bringing out more parts of your authentic self.

If you find yourself becoming resistant to making these changes or doing these things, please be kind to yourself, it may take a little time. When our body doesn't feel safe, we're naturally going to recoil, so if you feel like you need a little more inner work time around this than you thought – that's okay! As long as self-compassion and patience are at the top of your priorities list, your Inner Child will be patient back.

During the process, don't forget to celebrate your small wins and breakthroughs! This is new territory for this part of you, and a little self-praise goes a long way. Treat yourself to a little something nice, take yourself out for a fun walk somewhere, or simply tell yourself how great you're doing.

# Practical Exercise

For this Inner Child exercise, you're going to be writing letters from and to your Inner Child. Try to write them in a way that suits you, and allow the words to flow out. They don't need to be perfect, so if the words start pouring out and it becomes messy, you can either keep them how they are or rewrite them.

The first letter is from your Inner Child to your present self, with the suggested themes in mind:

- What did you struggle with the most in childhood?

- What made you feel scared or unsafe when expressing yourself?

- Where have you felt ignored in recent years?

- What things brought you joy that you would like more of now?

- What parts of yourself are ready to shine through again?

The second letter is from your present self back to your Inner Child after reading what your Inner Child wanted to say, with these suggested themes in mind:

- What have you struggled with most in adulthood, as a result of your childhood?

- How can you commit to creating safety for both the present version of you and your Inner Child so that you can start living in harmony?

- How can you commit to setting aside the time to give your Inner Child what it needs on a regular basis?

- What are you proud of your Inner Child and present self for?

End the letter with any supportive words or affirmations you'd like to say to your Inner Child.

53

# CHAPTER 4

# Clearing the Blocks & Reframing

Taking action and focusing on change is just as important as doing the digging into your shadow. I personally feel like this is the part that no one wants to talk about or teach, as it requires us to be consistent, brave and ruthless, showing up for ourselves day after day. This chapter is going to help you make the transition from awareness into action, and bridge the gap between what you've realised so far, and how to take practical steps to bring it into reality.

The main things we'll discuss in this chapter are:

- Revisiting old and outdated beliefs

- Putting some logic into why they're outdated and irrelevant to your here and now

- Techniques to grow with new, healthy beliefs.

Something I tend to see all too often is people who are doing the inner work and Shadow Work, but they get stuck on it for months and years on end. I've spoken to people who are so aware of their shadows, the work that needs to be done, where it all started and how it affects them in daily life, but they're stuck. What we need to remember during Shadow Work is that there is a very big difference between acceptance and enabling. Self-acceptance, which is a big part of Shadow Work, means that we look at what parts of our personality we have repressed, we accept that we may be flawed and remain open to all parts of who we are, but we look to change and work through the parts that are ultimately destructive to others and ourselves. Enabling, on the other hand, means we just continue to think and feel a certain way but make no real effort to change.

Self-acceptance isn't about digging up a bunch of stuff and then allowing ourselves to feel worse because we don't know what to do next. Being stuck like this means that it becomes our new zone of familiarity, or comfort zone, because there's a break in connection between awareness and taking action.

This is what we're going to be focusing on in the next few chapters, because ultimately, you want to feel like you're growing every day, showing up for you, rediscovering who you are and standing in your truth, right? We need action for that!

We have so much learned behaviour that ultimately needs overriding, which takes time. Our habits create real change, which is why it's important to partner up both inner work and external work. It takes us on average around two years of consistent habits and willingness to actually do the work for our brain to form new and independent patterns. I know two years sounds like a lot, but in the big picture of life, it's absolutely tiny!

## EXTERNAL PRACTICES

These can be anything outside yourself – your job, your environment, exercise, eating – but often, people struggle with seeing any growth from external practices, and I think I've worked out why this might be.

Think of it like this: You've seen on the internet or heard from a friend that positive affirmations and mantras are the key to changing your life. Everyone's doing it, you hear celebrities, influencers and so-called gurus talking about it, so it must work, right?

You do your affirmations and your mantras, and you hold out hope that if you just keep repeating them, they'll work. As you're repeating them to yourself, you feel yourself cringing beneath the surface and thinking something along the lines of "this is wishful thinking".

Our minds will recognise that we don't really believe what we're saying, and it will reflect in our energy, and ultimately, our lives and self-image. We are our own biggest BS detector in this work that we do, and eventually, it will catch up with us.

Over time, you feel like it's so surface level and you know deep down that it's not getting to the bottom of things for you, so you give up, maybe start again on and off, but become inconsistent with your growth overall.

Have you been in this situation? I know I have before I started doing my own Shadow Work!

What I will say though, is that although we can't rely solely on external practices, there is absolutely an element of "fake it till you make it" that comes in with reframing beliefs. We do have to create habitual change, and sometimes that means picking ourselves up day after day and embodying what we want to be until it becomes normal for us, whilst still being gentle with ourselves as we grow. However, without matching it up with inner work, we're just bypassing our emotions, our minds, our shadow and ourselves.

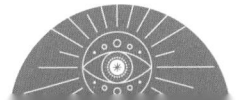

Our past seems so real to us in the present day because we're so used to being stuck there.

## INTERNAL WORK

I want you to try and relate what I'm saying to the negative beliefs that you stated in the Chapter 1 exercise. Most of the beliefs that we have are caused by a past opinion, experience, upbringing, social conditioning or something similar. It's actually quite bizarre to think that we spend so many years under a false illusion and false opinion of ourselves that was created by something other than us, isn't it?

The reason there's such a disconnect is because we never get taught to stand strong in our own beliefs, our own trust and our own confidence. We don't know when or how to use our discernment or question things, so we take opinions, experiences and conditioning as fact, which takes us a while to get out of.

But here's where I want you to question it. When you look at those beliefs that you first stated, and you traced them back to their root, and met with your Inner Child, do you see the clear pattern? Do you see that those opinions are merely a product of your past that your present self is clinging onto, purely because you have nothing else to replace it with?

If we don't have any reason to believe something other than what we've always been told, how on earth are we supposed to create change? It makes sense. Our past, even beyond trauma, seems so real to us in the present day – why? Because we're so used to being stuck there.

It's up to us to evolve, but if we don't explore new ways of thinking, question ourselves and create actionable steps, then of course we're going to be stuck. It's a bit like working in an office with no technology in a world where technology is necessary. It's going to be hard to communicate, with paperwork upon paperwork and things breaking due to them being old and outdated. It would be much easier, nicer and more comfortable to work in an office where you have the most up-to-date tech to allow you to do your job seamlessly, a comfortable place to sit, an environment that you can thrive in.

The difference between those two jobs in my analogy is that one of those offices has made the decision to evolve and create change, and one of them is choosing to be stuck in the past.

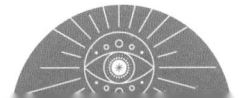

## REFRAMING

I want you to revisit your original beliefs and look into exactly why they aren't relevant to you now. We're going to interrogate your beliefs and dissect them to see which ones hold up under questioning. I know I've made it sound like an episode of *CSI*, but that's what I want you to think of it as. Our shadow is meant to be explored, we're supposed to have fun with it, experiment with it. After all, our Inner Child loves a bit of roleplay, don't they?

The reason I'm setting the scene as an interrogation is because I want you to experience the power being in your hands, not your beliefs. Your beliefs do not control you when you're in this space and doing this work, you are the one who has the upper hand, questioning your current beliefs and whether they have any relevance to your here and now.

I'll give you an example of my own when I first did this exercise, linking back to my earlier examples about childhood bullying and being a magnet for toxic people. One of my main beliefs that came up around this was the belief that I wasn't important enough or special enough to achieve anything beyond the basics, which I knew came from the blocks, patterns, feelings and so on, discussed in previous chapters.

When I first looked into this old belief and why it wasn't relevant to where I was in life, I realised that although I wasn't living up to my full potential, it wasn't a result of myself and my abilities, it was a result of what I had been told and how I had been made to feel about myself.

I had such low self-worth that I was under the control of a deep-seated belief that I could only achieve the bare minimum in life. Not only that, but that I was only worthy of being around people who treated me like dirt, because it was "normal".

When I realised this, amongst other things, I felt a rage that for so long, I had been living under this narrative. I started to then peel away the layers of my beliefs, unearthing more as I went along – like a domino effect.

I wrote something in my journal along the lines of, "This old belief isn't mine to hold, it was created by others who didn't have my best interests at heart, and they have no relevance in my life anymore. The belief that I can't achieve anything more than the basics and am not worthy of a good life stems from the emotional conditioning of others, and there's no difference between me and others that would result in me not being able to do big things in life and be happy. It's my responsibility to make it happen".

Once I reached the point of questioning my beliefs and working out why they weren't relevant to me here and now, I was able to focus on taking action, reframing my beliefs and changing habits. Whenever I did have a wobble or had a moment of low self-belief, I was able to remind myself about the cold hard facts of why it wasn't relevant to my present situation, and then replace it with the new habits and beliefs.

Like I said earlier, our minds need some sort of proof that our past is no longer in our present, proof that our new beliefs hold up somehow. This is exactly how we do it, and we rinse and repeat this as we go along.

Take one negative belief from the Chapter 1 exercise at a time and start to dissect the belief. Ask yourself:

- Where it comes from

- How it makes you feel

- How it has been stunting your growth and life as a result

- And most importantly, why it's genuinely not relevant in your life now.

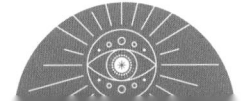

As you write the answer to the last point down, don't think too much about making it sound positive or enthusiastic. We want our brains to recognise it as a fact, not a goal, so the more simple you can make it sound, the better. It might be as simple as:

The belief that I'm ugly was caused by a toxic ex of mine, who always put me down for no good reason. It's not relevant to my present anymore as they're not in my life telling me that. It's up to me to accept and move on from the past, rather than keep it in my present.

Try it yourself – "the belief x isn't relevant to my present day because...":

Once you've done this with the beliefs that you previously wrote down, you can start to question your negative beliefs and their relevance as they come up in real time. Personally, I think the most powerful part of Shadow Work isn't the work that we sit down and plan to do (although we do need that part), but the alchemy that happens when you get into the habit of questioning yourself as you grow and experience different parts of life.

If there's one thing that I know for sure is that the more you grow, expand and do things that move you out of your zone of familiarity, the more shadows that come up that need addressing. You could be on a total upward trajectory, hitting all of your goals in life, feeling so connected with yourself, and have more parts of your shadow coming up than ever. That's a sign that you're growing.

A lot of people think that Shadow Work is a one-off process, but it's not. It's a lifelong journey that never stops. The only thing that changes is your ability to deal with things when they come up and your perception of your Shadow Self. Before I started my Shadow Work, I viewed those parts of myself as negative, bad and shameful. Now, those parts of myself are my biggest asset, they provide me with everything I need to continue returning home to myself and moving forward in life in my power.

It's important that you're gentle with yourself in the process of Shadow Work and reframing beliefs. Sometimes it can feel frustrating when we break habits, feel emotional or even when we try new things, but it's important to remember that it's all part of the process.

# Practical Exercise

For this exercise, I want you to take inspiration from what you wrote about why your old beliefs aren't relevant, and from that, create new beliefs to replace the old ones.

Draw a line down the middle of a page and on the left side write your old beliefs and on the right side, write your new, true beliefs. As you're writing these new beliefs down, make sure they're coming solely from you, not the influence of any ideals or expectations set by others.

After you've done this, you should now have the following to refer back to:

- Old and outdated beliefs

- Why they are not relevant in your present day

- New, true beliefs as a result.

63

# CHAPTER 5

# Creating Safety

Now that we've begun the work of reframing the beliefs that we always thought to be true, we're going to start digging even more. In the next few chapters, we'll be tapping further into your full self, and learning how to feel safe reintegrating your most wonderful and unique parts into your present.

Firstly, before we begin, let's just take a breather and celebrate how far you've already come on this Shadow Work journey. You're half way through this book, you've dug deep into some really heavy stuff and you've remained patient with your growth so far. Just take a few moments to really celebrate yourself here and all of the little (and big) shifts that you're making by doing this work.

This isn't always the most linear process, and everyone's Shadow Work is going to look different, because we all have such different lives, experiences and personalities. The process of reframing beliefs and reintegrating those repressed parts after realising why they're there can be a task within itself, as we've known those things to be true for so long.

## CREATING SAFETY

In order to make this all sustainable, we need to cultivate safety within ourselves so we can be expressive, independent and authentic. It feels foreign, right? Many of us, before starting Shadow Work, believe that if we unmask who we really are or express our unique qualities, we'll be persecuted. (I'll be going a lot deeper into why this is in the next chapter).

Most of us weren't brought up feeling that it was safe and okay to be ourselves, whether it was from parents, peers, teachers or all three. Most of us didn't feel accepted growing up and so now feel like we need to fit someone else's expectations.

This is why it's such a task to make these changes in adult life, because it's not what we're used to. You can bet that when I first started creating safety within myself and having my own back, I had all sorts of old stories running away with me, making me feel guilty for setting boundaries and being kind to myself. It was almost like I had withdrawal symptoms from my false persona and unhappiness. This is something that a lot of us go through, but we need to persevere and stay afloat during the changing tides.

If it does feel difficult or foreign at any point, just remember that simply accepting it as a part of the process and giving yourself extra room is a start in creating safety within yourself.

## SAFETY IN THE MIND

So, what do I mean when I talk about creating safety? When I talk about creating safety in the mind, I'm in part, linking back to our Inner Child and reparenting ourselves. As I mentioned in Chapter 3, we essentially need to give ourselves what we never had growing up. We need to recognise it, accept it and then create an action plan on how you're going to give back to yourself.

You need to set realistic boundaries, goals and tasks for yourself, but creating safety also involves backing yourself up when you feel like you're having a wobble, validating the things you have achieved and giving yourself support on your down days when you don't feel great.

Creating safety for yourself, especially when you're doing vulnerable inner work, is so important and this very much means not shaming yourself at any point. We all have an inner critic that sometimes turns up with a message, but we also have another side of our inner critic that seemingly knows no bounds unless we set them. It's so easy to fall into the trap of thinking nasty things and saying nasty things to ourselves.

We make a little error at work and it's "I'm such an idiot, sorry", or you look at yourself in the mirror in a dress that you tried on and it's "I hate my body". It's so habitual to shame ourselves and talk to ourselves like trash. Why is it that we live in a society that accepts it as normal when we hurl insults at ourselves, but when we begin to love ourselves and say kind things, it's looked down on?

## SAFETY IN THE BODY

Creating safety in the body, to me, is all about slowing down. We are living in a fast-paced and pretty stressful modern world, and it can feel really intense at times. We end up adapting to it and becoming walking cortisol machines, just feeling like we can't catch a break.

I hear from people a lot that they just don't have the time to slow down. At one point in my life, this was all I told myself: "I'm just too busy" or "I have way too much on my plate right now to slow down, I can't". I know now that for me, it was a case of me knowing what would happen if I did slow down and catch a break. It would get me thinking, wondering and being vulnerable with myself, and I was so far down the rabbit hole of being a corporate woman at that point, that even the thought of it made me cringe.

We all say we don't have enough time, but I have a little challenge for you, with the mindset of not shaming yourself, but simply learning from and working with yourself.

- Look at your phone settings and look at the collective screen time per day.

- Calculate how much of that time was spent on things that don't benefit you, like mindless scrolling on social media, even if it's just five minutes.

- Now, instead of scrolling, use those five minutes to check in with yourself, have a little breather, maybe you could even do some journaling.

- See if you can recognise anything else that's just become a habit because it takes your mind off things, like watching hours of TV in the evening.

- Can you take half an hour or even an hour out of that time to do something for you? You could nurture your body, meditate, go for a walk or simply feel reconnected to yourself for a little while.

- Try this for a month and watch how both your life and your perspective change.

So, creating safety in the body is all about slowing down and allowing yourself the time to give back to yourself, to become more aware of the present, and put things into perspective as a result. Creating safety in the body also allows us to look after our nervous system and our bodies so that we're not constantly stuck in fight or flight all the time.

## EXTERNAL VALIDATION

All of these things work as a domino effect with each other, and makes the entire process of Shadow Work a lot more beneficial. As you do these things more often, you'll start to create more safety in yourself, which as a result, will enable you to trust yourself more. Self-trust is what connects us to our intuition, it's what allows us to question our inner critic and to move past our blocks. However, creating self-trust often involves releasing the need to get the answers from someone or somewhere else.

I used to shut myself off to a lot of things in life because I was convinced that I just couldn't do certain things or that I wasn't knowledgable enough. I used to assume that everyone else had the answer, and worse, I used to crave hearing that answer from someone else. Now, we all fall back into this from time to time in many different ways. External validation on many levels is so deeply and inherently built into us, so it takes time to work through the constant need for it.

69

I'm going to be realistic here – who doesn't love to be told that what they're doing is good? I love it when my clients and my community tell me that my work is helping them, it makes me feel great and I love to hear that my work is fulfilling its purpose with others. But, do I rely on it as a source of my own worth? Absolutely not. The difference here is external validation is nice to have and not a necessity.

We're going
to be the ones
to disrupt the
structure by doing
Shadow Work.

We start to lose our personal power when we rely on external validation because we don't trust ourselves, value ourselves or believe in ourselves, which is why it's important to get into the habit of creating that validation for yourself.

Again, it all links back to reparenting the Inner Child, self-encouragement, checking in with yourself and being your own best cheerleader! Even if you have all of the external validation in the world it will expire at some point, which is why you need to sustain it within yourself.

Getting out of the habit of asking for everyone's opinion and advice on things is one of my absolute golden nuggets with this. When I started doing this and becoming aware of how much I was asking for, basically, permission from other people to do what I wanted to do, I was quite shocked.

So, over the next few weeks, start practising giving yourself the answers, and when you feel yourself looking for external validation or answers, first ask yourself is this really something you need help with, or can you do this by creating safety in yourself and digging into it alone?

Now, I'm not saying that you should completely isolate yourself from having discussions and listening to opinions of others, because that would result in us being closed minded, but what I am saying is to get into the habit of trusting yourself first.

## EXTERNAL NEGATIVITY

Look at how you can set certain boundaries with those around you who make you feel like you're moving backwards rather than upwards (we all have them somewhere in our lives).

The thing I see happening with many people is family members, friends or colleagues start to question the decisions they make and the things they do once they commit to their growth. Sometimes, this comes from genuine care and concern, other times it can come from jealousy, and often, it can just come from a place of projection.

People tend to project their own concerns onto us because they subconsciously know they wouldn't be able to do it. So when someone says to you, "Are you sure you want to do that, it doesn't seem like you'll be able to...", a lot of the time, what they really mean is, "I don't feel like I would be able to do that, it scares me". Again, this isn't always black and white, and people don't always come from a place of malice with this, but it is important to set a boundary around it so you can continue creating safety within yourself.

When you do get the feeling of someone crashing your party with a statement or question, take a step back and recognise that ultimately, this will be your decision, whatever happens. If it's something you think is coming from a place of genuine concern, you can of course be open to the discussion and conversation, but the key is to not let it define you.

# Practical Exercise

This exercise is something a little different but one that you'll be able to do in five minutes each day, to start cultivating safety in your mind and body.

Below is a Recognise code for you to scan. It will take you to a video of me guiding you through an EFT tapping exercise.

If you're new to EFT (emotional freedom technique) tapping, it is essentially a way of reconnecting to your body and mind, reinforcing positive beliefs, clearing the energy flow in the body and repairing the nervous system. It works by combining tapping the acupressure points on the body with affirmations.

I personally love EFT tapping because it gets us used to speaking kindly to ourselves and giving ourselves validation, which you may currently feel blocked with, as well as allowing us to tailor it to what we may be moving through with our inner work.

I'll guide you through the entire process and you'll be able to replay it each day.

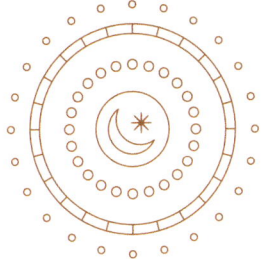

# CHAPTER 6

# Learning to be Seen Authentically

When you think about being seen as your most raw, vulnerable, authentic self, what comes up?

What about when it comes to openly standing up for what you believe in, your passions and your truth, even if it's not popular with those around you?

Fear? Excitement? Shame? Passion?

Our fear of being seen authentically manifests in so many different ways, and it goes further back than you may realise. In this chapter, I'm going to take you on a little journey through history to understand why we inherently fear being seen independently and authentically, beyond what we know about our present lives.

There are so many routes our lives can take, decisions we choose to make and people we decide to associate with due to having this deep-rooted fear within us. Often, the limits and blocks we have in our lives, on some level, all route back to the fear of being seen and stepping out into the world. There's a part of our psyche that does this on autopilot, but what if I told you there was something much deeper than that going on?

## THE WITCH WOUND

This term is being used more and more, and essentially links to our fear of being seen authentically, powerfully and spiritually. The witch wound is a generational wound that goes much deeper than our psyche, it's in our DNA, passed down from the generations before us who were persecuted for speaking their truth and being different. Scientists have now backed up the idea that trauma can be inherited, and the witch wound specifically carries the feeling of fear from notable times in history such as the witch trials.

You remember briefly learning about the witch trials in school, right? My school merely brushed over it in history class with very little care and then moved on. This seems odd to me in hindsight considering the huge number of people that were killed. Many people assume that those hung, burned and killed during the trials were women accused of practising witchcraft and magick. This wasn't the case. The trials went on for an astonishing 300 years in total, and victimised marginalised groups such as women (mostly), but also poor people, elderly people, vulnerable people and those who associated with them. People were accused of being witches for no logical reason, and it was a complete dog-eat-dog time. People accused others of being witches to protect themselves and their own families, people blamed others for their dying crops and bad weather because witches had supposedly cursed the land. A surprisingly small minority of people killed were keepers of the old ways, users of plant medicine, working with the power of nature, but the vast majority were just people falling victim to the mass hysteria caused by the church and the patriarchy.

The trials also targeted anyone who spoke out of turn against anything they disagreed with from the church or power structures at the time, which says a lot about our fear around speaking up for what we believe in!

*The witch trials were not a war on witches, they were a war on outsiders.*

I won't get into the complete details of the European or other witch trials, as that's for a whole other book, but the underlying issues of the witch trials and surrounding events still resonate deeply in our world today.

As the witch trials went on for so long, we have multiple generations worth of trauma all passed down from that time period – that's a lot! I've done a lot of research on this topic over the years, (unsurprisingly, there seems to be a very small amount of information that is available to find around this time in history, along with many inaccuracies taught in schools), and the more I started to dig, the more I started to find that the witch wound relates to those not wanting to be seen in their power, connected to their spirituality, nature and their authenticity.

## INHERITED AND PRESENT TRAUMA

The fear of stepping out on your own in the world, disagreeing with your peers or acquaintances, and being unique, goes even further back than I first thought. We've always naturally been in systems of some sort as human beings. We can trace this back to when we were in tribes and communities thousands of years ago. The fear of being ousted, persecuted and shut down for stepping out of those tribes and communities is something we've always felt very deeply throughout the course of history.

So, historically, we have a huge amount of inherited trauma that is stored deeper than our psyche, in our body. This is something that many of us will never actually figure out, it's like an itch that you just can't scratch, but when you find it and then start to work with it to release yourself from it, it's like the missing piece to the puzzle falling into place.

Amongst all of this inherited trauma, we also have our present trauma. The childhood bullying, the upbringing that tells you that you have to be a certain way, societal expectations. All of these things and more shape the way we end up in our adult lives, and for a lot of us, that leaves us wanting to rediscover who we really are as a result of hiding our true selves out of fear.

The idea that if you step out of your tribe or community, you will be "exiled" plays out in almost every mainstream area of life. Friendship groups, religion, society in general, even the cult-like corporate mentality! We grow up with this way of thinking, it gets drilled into us from such a young age, so no wonder we have such a hard time unlearning it.

## MOVING THROUGH THE FEAR

All of this works as a collective force that causes us to repress who we really are and become fearful of showing ourselves to the world.

Living inauthentically can really take its toll after a while. I know it did for me. I was absolutely exhausted in my younger years from constantly trying to mask who I was, fit in with the crowd and not be seen as myself. By hiding who we are, it can send us in completely the wrong direction in life, causing so much confusion and anxiety because we know deep down that things aren't aligned.

So, how can you recognise when this shows up for you? Where are you fearful of stepping out of line, of unmasking who you are or not sticking to the norm?

Putting ourselves out there, whether it's with our overall personality, our work, our beliefs or anything else, can feel daunting. The fear of being shut down in some way is bound to play up, and the truth of it is, you probably will get shut down, disagreed with or made aware of someone's opinion at some point… and that's okay.

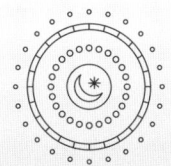

Being seen as your most raw self is a choice that may feel uncomfortable to begin with, but will allow you to move away from the exhaustion of living behind a mask.

If we try to wrap ourselves in cotton wool and protect ourselves from that inevitable thing, we only continue hiding. So, I suppose rather than moving through the fear itself, it's more about moving through the fear of being seen by standing strong in who you are, so that when you are faced with something uncomfortable, you'll be more than capable of handling it with confidence.

Being seen as your most raw self is a choice that may feel uncomfortable to begin with, but will allow you to move away from the exhaustion of living behind a mask.

This next exercise will help you to practise moving though the fear of being seen. It's important that you make sure you're allowing yourself to be your own safety net, as we went through in the last chapter.

As you're journaling, remember to take your time and revisit the exercise as many times as you need. You can do the prompts for multiple areas of life, separately or together. Once you're done, keep the affirmation part of the exercise handy so you'll always have access to it (such as on your desk or in your purse).

# Practical Exercise

These journal prompts will dig into where fear is currently showing up in your life, how it links to structures we're all conditioned with, and how you can move past it to live as you.

- What parts of yourself do you feel most insecure or scared about sharing out of fear of becoming an outcast?

- Are there any societal ideals or expectations that you can relate this feeling to, such as gender stereotypes, body and beauty standards or work expectations?

- Are there any past experiences that you can relate this to, where you were told you had to hide this part of yourself?

- What small but effective action point can you commit to doing each day or each week that will allow you to express this part of yourself more, cultivating more confidence?

**AFFIRMATION**

Now, you can mix all of these together, creating your own personal affirmation:

Even though I have been fearful of showing x part of myself, and I recognise that the reason behind that is x, I am free and safe now to not only welcome but express this part of myself to the world because x.

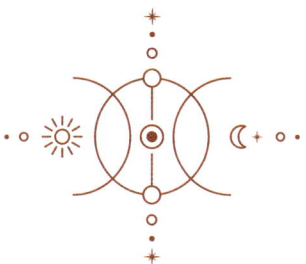

# CHAPTER 7

# Integrating Your Shadow Self

When we look at our Shadow Self and Shadow Work, we need to look at all parts of it. As I've mentioned earlier in the book, it's so important that we dig past the surface, and at times, revisit some uncomfortable places. Not only that, but we need to recognise that we may also have genuinely destructive parts of ourselves that we need to work on.

All too often in spiritual work, personal work and indeed, Shadow Work, I see a lack of accountability being taken for the very real parts that we all have that are damaging to ourselves and others. These could be behaviours and patterns we have picked up, learned or been exposed to that have stuck with us. What we don't want to get into the habit of is bypassing our damaging parts by saying "this is me and I shouldn't have to change any of it". Whilst, yes, this is true when it comes to your authentic traits, we need to separate that view from the things that need to be worked on.

In this chapter, we're going to look at:

- Recognising the genuinely destructive parts of yourself that need to be worked on

- Separating the destructive traits from your authentic traits

- Integrating your authentic Shadow Self

- Expressing your full self.

## SPOTTING THE DIFFERENCE

It can be difficult to differentiate between destructive parts that need to be worked on, and the unique and authentic traits that are inherently a part of you (which sometimes still may not be typically desirable things, and that's okay).

So, the question that may be in your mind right now is "how do I tell the difference?"

This is one of the hardest questions to answer, as this work will be different for everyone, and honestly, it can be difficult, especially if you're someone who doesn't have much self-trust right now. This was a mountain I once had to climb too.

At one point in my life, I was so used to being under the thumb of the opinions and expectations of others, I didn't know what things I actually needed to work through and what I should be celebrating about myself. After all, I was told that my passion, my humour and my creative mind were all "problems", but I couldn't do my work today without any of these things!

It takes time and compassion, and I won't sit here and tell you that you'll know exactly what's what right away, as you'll need to take the time to get to know yourself more deeply as you continue this journey. But one thing I will say is that as long as you meet yourself where you're at, treat your Inner Child and all parts of you with patience and compassion, and practise having your own back with no judgment, you'll be able to see these things a lot more clearly.

At this point, I feel it's important for me to be mindful of trauma, as there are so many of us who have gone through emotional conditioning around this, which is ultimately what creates our repressed parts. Although Shadow Work is something that equips you to look at your shadow alone, please don't hold back from seeing a therapist, coach or a mentor if you feel like you need a listening ear around these things.

A great way to begin to figure out the difference between what's actually destructive and what's really just us being authentic is to ask yourself one very important question:

*Is this something I can see or feel affecting me and others negatively, or is it something I have gotten used to believing is wrong because of being told it is by someone else?*

## REPRESSED AUTHENTIC TRAITS

I'll give you an example from my own story. A trait that I was told I needed to repress was my passion. When I looked back at who was telling me that I just needed to keep my head down, stay quiet and stop feeling passionate, it was always people who wanted power or control. I started to realise that if my passion was there to be used for the good of myself and others, why on earth would I tone it down?

Those who want to dim your light to make theirs seem brighter will convince you that staying quiet is better for you in some way.

## DESTRUCTIVE TRAITS

A destructive part of myself that I had to work through was my anger. I used to get very angry at one point in my life and it was clearly affecting me and those around me.

I didn't work through this part of myself by going to anger management or going into one of those rage rooms where you smash stuff up (although it does look quite therapeutic!). I dug even deeper than that to work out why I had such a short fuse. I took a good look at the life I was living at the time and worked out that I was so frustrated because I didn't have anything that fired me up. I was surrounded by people and things that made me feel like a rat in a cage, just clawing to get out and do my own thing. As a result, I became very self-destructive and angry, affecting me and the ones I loved.

By taking a closer look at this destructive trait, I learnt my anger wasn't some inherent part of me and it could be worked through. I met myself with compassion and changed what needed to be changed in my environment, whilst I also took accountability for my own actions and inner work at the same time.

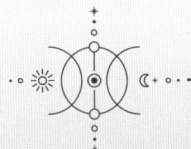

Those who want
to dim your light
to make theirs
seem brighter will
convince you that
staying quiet is better
for you in some way.

When we start to look at the genuinely destructive parts of ourselves with the mindset of, "Okay, this is what I can work through to make life feel better" rather than "I'm always doing something wrong" or "I'm such a horrible person", we're able to work on these things in a sustainable way. Throwing a pity party and indulging in self-loathing about things that we need to work through does nothing for us or anyone else. If you're doing this type of inner work and consciously working through these parts, then that's something to be proud of! Just give it time and patience.

One element to consider here is that a destructive trait might stem from having to repress your authentic traits. Using my example, the anger I was feeling stemmed, in part, from the frustration of repressing my passion and not living the life I wanted. Going deeper into my shadow and working on these parts of myself allowed me to work this out.

## FIGURING IT OUT

Over time, and the more you dig into aspects of yourself, the easier it will be to distinguish between destructive and authentic traits, even if it doesn't seem obvious right away.

So, let's go back to this question again…

*Is this something I can see or feel affecting me and others negatively, or is it something I have gotten used to believing is wrong because of being told it is by someone else?*

…what comes up for you? What answer did you give to question 6 in Chapter 1: What parts of yourself can you openly recognise as destructive, imperfect or negative?

Sit with these for however long you need and see what shows up for you.

# INTEGRATION

Let's now take a look at integrating and welcoming in the authentic traits that are inherently a part of you, and if used correctly, can work as your superpower! Take a look back at the authentic traits that you have repressed by revisiting your answers to question 9 in Chapter 1.

Usually, our inherent traits tend to get repressed in childhood, or whenever we start to feel like we're unsafe in some way to express them. So, I want you to try and revisit your Inner Child again here, and remember what made you different or quirky as a child, and if you can, remember when those things started to be seen negatively.

Were you, like me, the typical "weird kid" or was there perhaps a specific reason that you felt like you had to be silent with your self-expression?

When we recognise things that we have repressed, it's not an overnight job to get them back and start integrating them into our life again. It comes with creating safety, and ultimately, getting into the habit of not wearing the mask we've worn for so long.

Are there perhaps traits from your inner teen that you hid away coming into adulthood, which you can recognise as an important yet forgotten part of you? When we start coming into our teens, a whole new world opens up for us, usually only to have it shut right back down by being told we shouldn't be certain ways and we have to fit in.

Start building on your traits by revisiting multiple times in your life looking at how you've grown into who you are today, and looking at what traits have been hidden for the sake of others. Writing it all down helps, perhaps in bullet points if that's what you find easier.

Expressing all of this can be a task for many of us, and as I mentioned, it absolutely takes time. But, we need to drip-feed it in somehow, otherwise we would just be recognising all of the traits we repress without taking action on welcoming them back in.

Integrating and expressing your Shadow Self can feel unsafe for us because our mind is instantly going to link back to what happened the first few times we expressed certain parts of our personality. This is why creating safety is essential, and if you need a reminder on how to create safety within yourself whilst you're drip-feeding the self-expression in, then head back over to Chapter 5.

## REDEFINING JUDGMENT

Self-expression only feels scary to us when we haven't already cultivated this safety, and a big part of that is owning your authenticity when people don't like you. The primary reason we don't express who we are is because we fear judgment, and the truth of all of this is: there will always be people out there who judge you – but that's okay!

My mother used to tell me, "You can't be everyone's cup of tea when you're champagne." I absolutely love this saying because it speaks to the truth of life, which is if you worry about being liked by everyone, you're not actually able to flourish as you. You're not going to be everyone's cup of tea, because you're champagne – some people hate champagne and some people love it. Some people hate tea and some people love it.

As soon as you begin to get comfortable with the fact that people's judgment of you is more of a reflection of how they feel about themselves and the world around them, and not really about you, it becomes a lot easier to shamelessly express who you are.

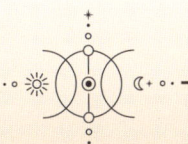

You can't be
everyone's
cup of tea
when you're
champagne.

I, of course, had this experience in the broader context of life, but even when I started doing my spiritual work. I felt like an outcast at times because I'm not your stereotypical spiritual person. I'm not overly into my crystals, I'm quite a hyperactive person, I swear like a sailor, sometimes I wear long flowy flower dresses, and other times I wear Iron Maiden t-shirts to my events and workshops. But, I didn't get into the industry to impress others or worry about judgment, I got into the industry after doing the deeper work to rediscover and express who I am, and to help others move through their personal development, leading with my heart and encouraging others to lead with theirs.

You deserve to express who you are. You deserve to live a life where you can freely and wholeheartedly wake up each day and feel like yourself, without a mask. But it's only you that can create that reality.

Let's round this chapter off with a week-by-week self-expression action plan. This exercise is going to be focused on drip-feeding in your self-expression, whilst creating safety so that it can be long lasting.

# *Practical Exercise*

Each week, set yourself one small daily action to allow yourself to connect with and outwardly express your repressed traits. This should be in a way that feels genuinely exciting and inspiring for you, so don't be afraid to think outside the box with this.

You may feel slightly uncomfortable when you first start to do this. From my own experience, I sometimes think it's best to just feel the discomfort of it in full force and more often than not, the more you do it, the more normal it will become – especially when you allow yourself to have genuine fun with it. The fun will outweigh the uncomfortable.

Here's how you can outline your weekly plan:

- Start with setting a goal for yourself, along the lines of, "My overall self-expression goal for this week is…"

- Make a note of small actions that you can take each day to achieve this goal.

At the end of the week, think about how you feel:

- Do you feel you've moved closer to the goal you started out with?

- What are you especially proud of yourself for?

- What would you like to improve on?

- How can you celebrate this week's achievement?

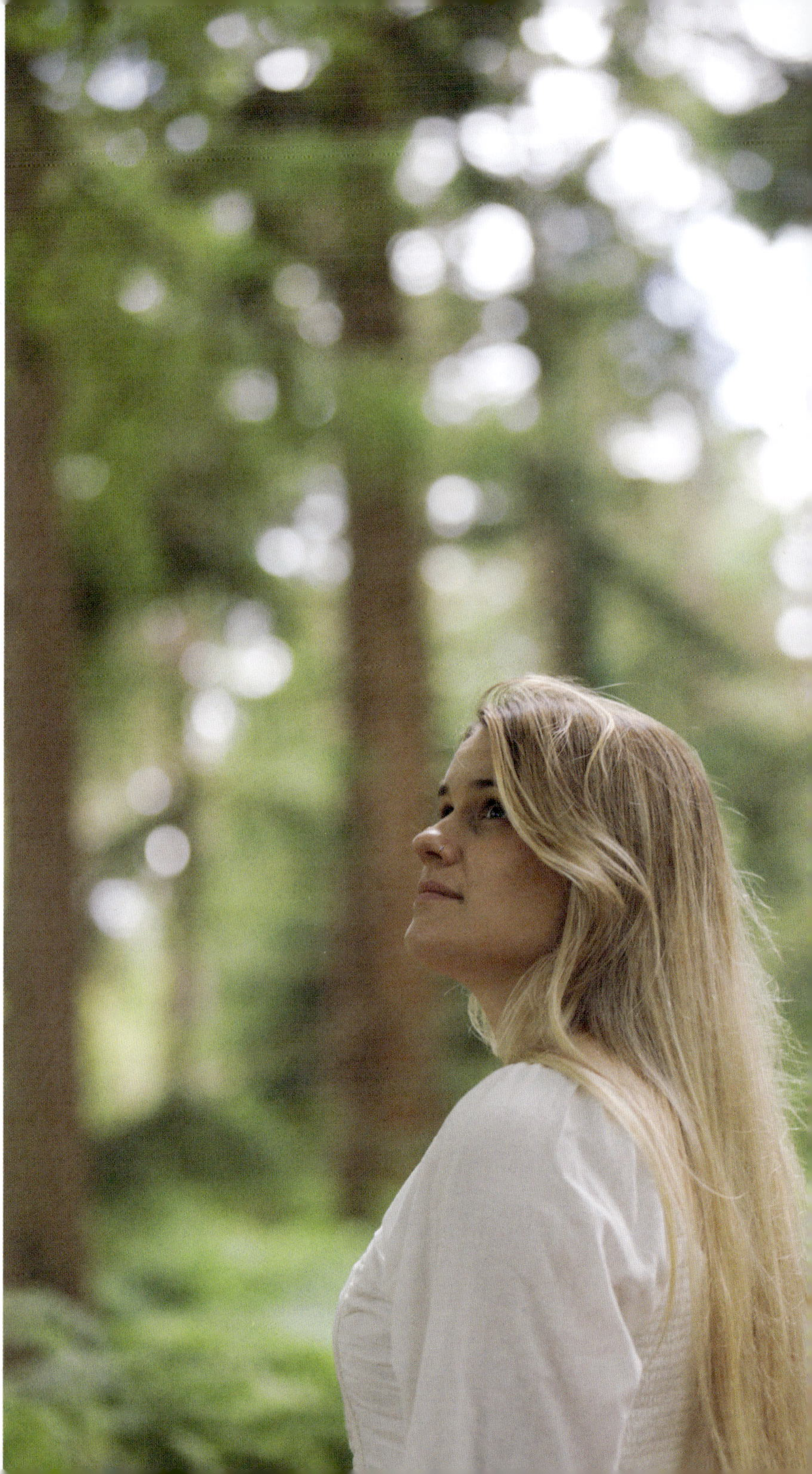

# CHAPTER 8

# Owning Your Story

Many of us see our past as a bit of a nuisance. It can feel like we have so much baggage to carry around, so much weight on our shoulders from something that doesn't even exist anymore, right? We may even do the work to gain closure from our past and then move on from it so we can detach and forget. After all, why on earth would you want to remember, talk about or celebrate awful things that have happened to you? In this chapter, I'm going to tell you exactly why.

*Your story is not separate from you – it never will be.*

After we go through things that leave us with scars, trauma or baggage, our first thought is to move on, but we don't actually take the time to look at ourselves in the situation, how we overcame those things and how it makes us even more equipped to share our wisdom.

We end up feeling so ashamed of ourselves, worried that others will judge us or view us differently if we choose to own our past rather than hide it. I used to be terrified that my past would somehow catch up with me because I was doing everything to hide it. I had a belief in my head that what happened to me was somehow my fault, and I should feel shame around it. I used to think that my past, because what happened to me was awful, was only there to bring me pain. I couldn't have been further from the truth.

## PERFECTION IS NOT REALITY

In today's world, we strive for this picture-perfect exterior that shows no blemishes, scars or imperfections. We feel like we can't drop the ball or let any of the cracks show. We have a world fuelled by social media where we can essentially create a double life for ourselves, showing the world what we want them to see, and keeping our true feelings bottled up, terrified that people will one day find out.

But, do you know what's also great about today's world? That amongst this reality, we also have an oddly contrasting reality where more people are talking about their stories than ever before, people are opening up, and owning their past. We never would have done that in previous generations, and I think that's beautiful.

It can be easy to forget that this exists in the same world where we need to be perfect, especially if part of the reason you feel shame around your story is due to how you were raised, as I think is the case for many people.

## TURNING PAST EXPERIENCES INTO POSITIVE ENERGY

I'm someone who believes that we go through a lot of things for a reason, and I think that often it's so that we can go on to help others, almost like a chain reaction. I remember being told that at one point in my life and thinking, "How on earth could that be true. They have obviously never been through something like this". Now, I see exactly why I went through certain events in my life.

Owning your story, realising how you have become the person you are today as a result, and taking it forward with you to do something impactful is the real magic.

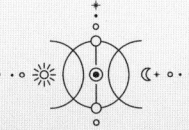

By hiding your story away, you're doing yourself and the world a disservice, which is why it's time to embrace it.

When I started to see how my purpose was to help others with their own Shadow Work, personal growth and fears, it became even more apparent to me that I couldn't hide my story. It was no longer just about me, it became about who I was doing it for and the change I wanted to create.

You may also start to feel this as you begin to own your story more, whether you're a teacher, a guide, a mother, a lover, a friend or just a listening ear. I believe that we all have a legacy of some sort to create from our own life experiences. It's just up to us whether we choose to hide that away out of the fear of judgment or reach the people who need us. By hiding your story away, you're doing yourself and the world a disservice, which is why it's time to embrace it.

If we weren't given a safe environment to talk about the things that have happened to us when they did, it creates the foundation of the shame we have to live with going forward, and it sticks with us. As a result of that, much like healing the Inner Child by reparenting ourselves, we need to create that safety and security for ourselves, rather than allowing that feeling to carry on into the present and future.

## REFRAMING YOUR STORY

So, how do you start to own your story? By reframing what your story has done for you.

I'm not a huge fan of the saying "everything happens for a reason". Truth be told, some things probably don't. I prefer "most things happen for a reason", but I suppose that's not as catchy is it? Even when things do happen for you, it's usually hard to see it at the time. But when we're looking at things in hindsight, I think that looking at what your story has done for you, and looking at what you're going to make of it, are absolutely crucial.

I want you to focus on the following questions:

- What are the messy parts of my story that I try to hide the most from myself and others?

- Even though some of these experiences were traumatic or uncomfortable, what can I recognise in hindsight that this has made me aware of/able to do/equipped me with?

- How can I start to own this part of my story more proudly?

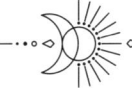

Reframing your story and owning all parts of it is about facing it head on. This can feel like foreign ground at the start, because you may have spent so long hiding it away, but it's the only way you'll be able to own all parts of it proactively.

The more we start to be honest with ourselves around this, the more the mask will start to come off. We mask different parts of ourselves, our stories, our true personality, our feelings, and it's only when we go into deeper layers of ourselves that the mask starts to crumble.

Unmasking takes time, and really, we probably all do a bit of masking from time to time, even when we've done the work, because we have to adapt to the world, that's a part of life! But the true unmasking that really matters is what happens when you start to be honest with yourself about who you are, your story and what you really want to do with it.

# Practical Exercise

For this exercise, we're going to get a bit more playful. I want you to imagine you are a protagonist in a movie or a superhero in a comic. We're going to be writing your origin story.

Every superhero has one, and it's time to start feeling like one yourself. Usually, the superhero has some sort of traumatic past. For example, Bruce Wayne lost his parents in a robbery when he was a young boy, and as a result, he became Batman and devoted his life to protecting Gotham City so he could minimise crime and suffering.

So, what's your origin story? Feel free to refer back to any previous pages or notes you've made from past exercises, and don't forget to have fun with this. Get creative and really play around with the idea of becoming the hero of your own story!

Here are some prompts to get you started:

- What's your superhero name or alias?

- What obstacle(s) have you had to overcome in your past?

- What emotions have you felt or moved through as a direct result?

- What is your special superpower relating to your past?

- How has your past equipped you to change the world, even if it's just your small corner of it?

Don't hold back with being creative in this exercise, tuning into your Inner Child, and as you go along, feel a sense of pride for everything you've accomplished!

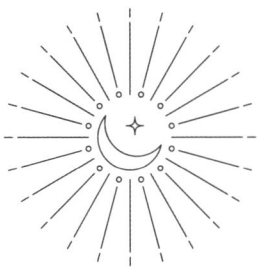

# CHAPTER 9

# Getting Out of Your Own Way

As you continue to move past what you've always believed to be true about yourself and see these beliefs as, usually, a reflection of the past, you start to question what more is possible for you in this life. What dreams and opportunities have you potentially been blind to because of these old beliefs and programming?

When I say dreams and opportunities, I mean anything from doing the work you love to simply living your life feeling a certain way – it varies depending on where your true will lies and what your heart really wants.

For me, Shadow Work was a serious wake up call that I was the only person standing in the way of what I really wanted in life: freedom. Freedom has been the one thing I have always craved, in every sense of the word. My work, my life, my emotions, all of it. I just wanted to feel like I could live life on my own terms, rather than under someone's thumb.

It's funny, actually, because I worked something out when I looked further into my shadows around the longing for freedom. I had this thing where I would go for jobs that I had absolutely no interest in, where I would be a doormat, and then I would leave after three months. That feeling of quitting and walking out the door, driving away and going home to my freedom gave me such a rush – I loved it! I kept going into jobs that I hated just so that I could quit to get this rush. It gave me the same feeling I used to get when I was a child and used to fake being sick so I could get picked up from school and spend the rest of the day at home, or when I was a teenager and used to do things because I loved the feeling of knowing I could get caught. Freedom to me now looks a lot different, and I experience the feeling of freedom each day simply by existing in the life I've built for myself.

I kept seeing this recurring theme in my life of the need for freedom, expression and individuality. It's how I knew that freedom was what I really wanted. In the first part of my twenties, I told myself that I just wanted a stable, high-paying job and that's all. I lied to myself for a long time because I wasn't doing the work to find out what it was that I really wanted out of life. When I did start Shadow Work, those repeating patterns of the need for freedom didn't come up so often early on, as I saw them as shameful rather than a part of me that could be channelled into something greater.

Ultimately, our goals change, and they'll continue to change and expand the more confident, brave and authentic we become.

## BEING HONEST WITH YOURSELF

So, after putting in all of the work you've done over your time reading this book...

## *What do you really want?*

This isn't a wish from a genie, so you don't have to answer this question with one singular and hugely impactful thing. Ultimately, our goals change, and they'll continue to change and expand the more confident, brave and authentic we become. But, right now, ask yourself, what is it that you really want? Is it a feeling? Is it a change of situation? Take a few moments just to pause and reflect on it and drop into your heart space to answer it.

If the concept of dropping into your heart space is new to you, then I invite you to practise connecting with your body. Take a few moments to close your eyes, take a few deep breaths, drop your shoulders and place your hands on your heart. Take a few minutes to just sit with yourself, releasing all judgment or expectations you have around what you should be doing or should be getting out of life, or even from this book, almost like the world is stopping just for a few brief moments. Connecting to your heart space is really just about having forgiveness for yourself, and allowing yourself to be vulnerable, opening up to the emotions that need to be heard. The more you can set aside the time to connect with yourself in this way, the more you'll start to work with yourself, free of judgment and barriers.

If you're still deeply in your comfort zone, you might find it difficult to answer this right now, which is fine. If you're drawing a blank, practise forgiving yourself and supporting yourself, rather than shaming yourself or questioning yourself. The answer to this question might come in bits over a period of time, or it might suddenly hit you like a freight train – just be open to it.

## OUR COMFORT ZONE

Our comfort zone resides within our ego. Our ego is a tricky part of our psyche which, if we don't set boundaries with it, can actually stunt your growth. Think of the ego like the overprotective parent. They think that they are doing what they're supposed to by protecting us, warning us about the dangers of life and advising us on what to do. However, when these things come up at inappropriate times, or with everything we experience, the dynamic changes from protective to overbearing and unhealthy.

Our ego has its comfort zone in our old beliefs, so when we change them, start to shed layers of past experiences and do new things, the ego pipes up, which is when our imposter syndrome comes in.

Imposter syndrome is that heavy voice within us that tells us all the reasons why we shouldn't be doing something. Why we shouldn't be seen, why we shouldn't do new things, why we shouldn't put ourselves out there, all linking back to the old beliefs that have been formed in the past.

As you step further out of your comfort zone, break down your own barriers and do new things, you can bet that imposter syndrome will rear its ugly head and tell you all of the reasons you shouldn't do it. This is where having boundaries with our ego and imposter syndrome comes in. In order to grow, we need to make sure we don't let the ego take hold 100 per cent of the time, and trust that we know what we're doing, even if we appear to fail sometimes.

## LEARNING TO FAIL

Approaching your goals with fearlessness comes with feeling okay to fail. When we were kids, we lived life through rose-coloured glasses, blissfully unaware of what could go wrong and the dangers that are out there. We weren't afraid to fall off our bikes or swing on the swing set really high. We were just totally immersed in it for the experience and enjoyment, not wondering about what may or may not go wrong as a result. We develop all of the fear when we move into adult life and start worrying about failure, judgment and not doing things right.

If you could meet your new goals and desires with that same fearless, childlike energy, and treat them with an inquisitive mindset that says "it's not that serious, I'm just having fun and exploring", then the process will feel a lot easier. The last thing we want to be doing is going ahead with all of this inner work only to be meeting ourselves on the other side with pressure and self-judgment. So, remember that this journey is for you, and you have the time to explore new facets of yourself and life – you're not in a time crunch!

Meeting yourself with this gentle and curious attitude is a huge part of getting out of your own way when it comes to figuring out what you really want and what your new goals are. It's all well and good setting out your new goals, but if you're going to do it by putting the wrong type of pressure on yourself, then it's not going to feel fun for you and will most likely send you straight back into your comfort zone.

In order for us to create lasting change in life, it's so important that we follow up our inner work with action and habit-changing that feels good, a little bit like positive reinforcement. Part of this is about becoming comfortable with experiencing new things and being open to change! When our comfort zone is our natural habitat, we stay there for as long as possible to make sure we don't have to experience anything different. Although our comfort zone can be more unhealthy than new experiences, it's usually easier for us to stay where we are.

Find out
what your
heart wants,
listen to it
and go for it.

## THINK BIG

When you're looking at setting out your new goals and rethinking your capabilities in line with what it is that your authentic self really wants, try to get out of the habit of thinking small.

Again, I'll use my work story as an example. Even when I first started doing my Shadow Work, and I thought I'd really broken through my layers to think big, I was still thinking small. (This is, of course, part of the process, as we always have smaller layers to break through first.) I realised that I wasn't being true to myself by working in the field I was working in, so I made it my mission to move departments – I wanted to be a part of the employee welfare team, looking after the people and creating happiness in the workplace. They didn't actually let me move departments in the end, which created the chain reaction of me doing my work today, which is very telling.

But I really thought I had it nailed with this one realisation and thought I'd found my purpose. All the while I was still working for a company where everyone was miserable and I got treated very poorly overall. My problem here was that deep down I still didn't think I was capable enough of doing what I really wanted to do, which was working for myself and helping others in my own unique way. I was still in my comfort zone and I was still very much avoiding what it was that I actually wanted.

So, my message to you when you are rethinking your capabilities is to not be afraid to zoom out a little. When we're so invested in our situations, it's hard to actually see possibilities outside of it. But I'm telling you that no dream is too big as long as it is genuinely coming from your heart. I personally wouldn't change how I went about that situation, because as I looked back on each layer I broke through to get to where I am, I see just how needed each one was, and I believe the same for you, too. I just wish I had known that what I wanted wasn't at all far-fetched like I was told in the past, which is why I'm here telling you!

# Practical Exercise

For this exercise, you'll be setting out your new goals and matching each one up with four or five action points you know you'll need to do to get there. You'll be breaking it down even further with a monthly, weekly and daily plan that you'll review month by month. To finish, you'll set out an affirmation to remind yourself why it makes sense that you can absolutely achieve it.

It's important we put energy and action into what we want. Despite what social media will have us think, nothing is ever effortless. We don't just set out manifestations and have things fall into our laps, but it can be a hell of a lot of fun when doing something from the heart.

Set out the following at the beginning of the month:

- Your goal

- Action points

- How can I build this into my day?

- How can I build this into my week?

- How can I build this into my month?

To create the affirmation, we want to focus on logic, as we're retraining ourselves to see this as the new norm. So, your affirmation could look a little like this: "It makes absolute sense that I'm going to achieve the goals I set out this week, because I have set aside the specific time to take the action steps that will get me there. I'm proud of myself for setting myself up for real success!".

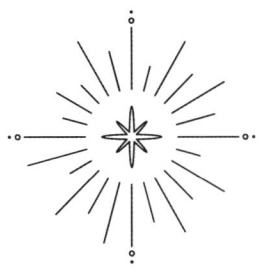

# CHAPTER 10

# Creating Lasting Change

You've done some incredible work over the last few chapters that have been largely focused on action, which can often be the hardest part. The next stage is all about implementing it in your own time. Hopefully, with the action plans set out in this book, you'll be able to do just that!

We've covered a huge range of inner work, from simply bringing awareness to where you are now and your current beliefs, tracing it all back and reframing these beliefs, meeting with your Inner Child and repressed parts of yourself and finally, to putting it all into practice by creating a proactive plan. Over the next few months, you can continue this work and refer back to everything we've covered along the way.

In this final chapter, I'll be going over the following things to make sure you're fully prepared to continue your Shadow Work journey:

- Embracing and welcoming change

- Recognising self-sabotage and old patterns returning

- Finding the balance between keeping yourself on your toes and being gentle with your journey.

## PREPARE FOR CHANGE

As I've mentioned before, it's important to set yourself up to expect change. Sometimes, change can feel quite uncomfortable, especially when we're not used to it. If there's one thing that I've learned on my Shadow Work journey it's that change is inevitable. When we start to work with anything internal, no matter what it is, it will somehow reflect on the external. It can feel a little bit like Pandora's box after you start to delve into Shadow Work, but in the most beautiful way. Any change I've felt after doing this work, even if it felt uncomfortable at times, I knew it was happening to allow me to start a new cycle or level up in some way.

I love the term level up to describe what we go through – it's like points represent the life lessons we have to go through before we can reach the next stage, or level, in our life. Usually when we do level up, it can feel turbulent, but that's part of the excitement when you start to experience it more and more, because even if it's painful in some way, you know it's about to get really freaking good on the other side!

I always like to do a little bit of reflection and give thanks for what I've learnt when I'm over the other side of the hill, to really bring awareness to what I've learned from the previous cycle. I would recommend you do this too.

## FALLING BACK AND MOVING FORWARD

It can be very easy to get scared by all this and revert back to old patterns of being in your comfort zone. If you feel yourself doing this, go back through the chapters you feel you need to revisit. We're all human, however, and we all go back into our comfort zones from time to time, and we can't beat ourselves up entirely for it. But, what we can do is recognise when it happens, sit with ourselves, look at why we went back, and then create action going forward.

Prepare yourself to put in some shifts — you've got this!

As we continue this Shadow Work journey, we don't want to be ignoring anything, including falling back into old habits. Many people just bypass how they feel or why they did something because they get frustrated. Instead of feeling frustrated or shaming yourself, use reverting back to old patterns as a learning opportunity to figure out why it happened. This will allow you to create lasting change by really understanding yourself more deeply.

Remember, there are no "old versions" of you. There's you, there are things to integrate and there are things to work through. Integrating your Shadow Self and taking off the mask can take time, but as long as you're taking small steps towards it, then you're doing the work. The same goes for working through the parts that are destructive – it's not an overnight job, and that's okay. Be patient with your progress.

It can take time to find the balance between pushing yourself outside of your comfort zone and being gentle with yourself. My advice for how to go about the next few months would be to forgive yourself but keep yourself accountable. The last thing we want to do is fall into the pattern of enabling ourselves, which is quite easy to do at times. We want to be taking accountability for our growth, but in a way that feels encouraging rather than negative.

When we get into the habit of reminding ourselves that it's okay for us to come back to a new place of safety that isn't our usual comfort zone, but is actually a place where we can still continue to grow by doing this work, we'll start to feel more familiar and secure with it.

Our comfort zones will forever be changing whilst we do this work, but that's exactly why we need to become okay with adapting to change. When the time comes for us to move on because we've outgrown our current stage, we'll need to move on from our current comfort zone at the same time.

On the next few pages, you'll find my top tips to take with you on your Shadow Work journey.

## Question yourself at every chance you get.

The thing about Shadow Work is that it needs constant renewal. It needs us to question ourselves so that we can start to unpick the things that come up for us. So, if you feel a limiting belief or imposter syndrome flaring up, stop, sit with it and question it. Our ego doesn't expect us to put it on the spot and start questioning it, because it doesn't come from a place of logic, it comes from a place of habit. Logic is so important for us as it allows us to make sense of things, and in turn, trust it. So when a certain belief, block or shadow comes up and we question why it's there, we need to identify the belief, trace it back, make sense of it by seeing how it's not relevant, creating logic from that, and creating self-trust as a result so that we can go forward without the imposter syndrome.

## Remember that this is continuous.

Shadow Work isn't something you'll do once and leave behind, it's a skill that we practise for the rest of our lives and master along the way. The more we grow, change and have new life experiences, the more shadows are going to be created or brought to the surface. The only difference is that when you don't know how to do the Shadow Work, those things can end up taking hold and leading you down the wrong path. Or you can have those same things playing out, and you'll be able to grow from them because you do your Shadow Work. The key is to remember that just because things may feel a little rocky at times in the future, it doesn't always mean you're going backwards, it just means that new things are coming up to be worked through!

## Patience, patience and more patience.

I know I've said this before, but it's just so important. As with anything that grows, whether it's a plant, a baby, a business, a family – our personal journey needs to be nurtured too. If you feel you're getting frustrated with yourself or shaming yourself because something didn't go the way you expected it to, just remember that you're new to this. Again, using the Inner Child as an example, you wouldn't get frustrated with a child version of you or your own child if they were trying their absolute best at something and made a little mistake. You'd encourage them, tell them to dust themselves off and keep going. This is exactly the stance you should be taking with yourself, too.

## Don't get so fixated on an end goal that you bypass the journey.

Whether you set yourself a practical goal about some sort of change you want to make, or a more emotional goal around how you want to feel, it's important not to obsess over the end goal so much that it takes away from the beauty of your journey. I see people doing this on a fairly regular basis. They either fixate and attach their worth to something like work, and they say, "I'll finally be my best self when I've got my business up and running" or "I'll finally be fully healed when...". Shadow Work isn't about being your best self all the time or being fully healed. It's about learning how to get in touch with all parts of you to work out what's actually going to make you feel fulfilled, so don't get caught up in focusing on a future version of yourself.

## *Have fun with your self-expression.*

Your self-expression needs to feel somewhat good for you (even when it's uncomfortable). It's no good trying to force yourself into a situation where you feel completely out of place and that you don't find fun. Try and drop into your creativity a little and ask yourself what would feel like a fun way to get creative, to start being yourself, without completely hiding away from the rest of the world. The reason it makes a difference when it feels fun is because the feeling of fun links to our authenticity, and the dopamine release that we get in the process will make us want to come back to do it more – this is how habit changing starts off! So, have fun, get creative and do something that lights you up.

## *Wake up your Inner Child.*

Working with your Inner Child is something I would recommend to just about anyone. Our Inner Child is in there, and they want to be heard. When we're ignoring it, we feel it, but when we actually make the effort and set aside the time to connect with that part of us, we connect back to what once made us feel alive, allowing us to be more creative, open and free in our everyday lives. Combine your self-expression with your Inner Child work from time to time, too!

## Meet with different parts of you.

It's not just your Inner Child that needs to be heard, we also have our inner teen, and really, any inner part of ourselves that is connected to a major time in our lives. These parts of us will likely be felt more when we go through specific things, and when this comes up for me, I like to reflect on what the situation is, how this inner part of me can help and how I can thank her for teaching me what I know.

## Record your progress.

I wish I had recorded more progress from my Shadow Work journey – it's my one and only regret with it all. Whether it's journaling, video diaries or something else, I would absolutely recommend recording your progress as it allows you to see how far you've come. We so often get caught up in the here and now, thinking we're only making slow progress, when really, we just don't realise how much progress we've made. When you record a video diary or journal things down, it means you can look back when you're feeling like you are making slow progress, and remind yourself how amazing you're doing. It can be quite incredible to see the difference with only two or three months of work.

### *Allow yourself some time away from Shadow Work.*

This one is important, even more important than allowing yourself to have fun in this process. Allow yourself some time to get out of your own head. There seems to be this expectation with personal and spiritual development that we must always be on it and we have to be squeaky clean all of the time otherwise we've fallen off the wagon. I can't bear this rhetoric and I can't stress enough how important it is to just have a day every now and again where you can just go and do something else. I spend most of my days in my little countryside cottage, being in nature, doing my soul-led work, trying to stay off social media, not watching the news or any live TV, but you can bet that when I go somewhere on holiday, the TV goes straight on and I'm watching some trashy reality show in the hotel room. Why? Because our minds, our bodies and our souls just need a break sometimes! We're all human, aren't we? It's okay for us to watch some trashy TV or eat some fast food now and again, and just have a little regular cheat day from personal work – so go for it!

### *Celebrate your wins, both big and small.*

Just like recording your progress, practise being present in your journey. Celebrating your wins and getting used to praising yourself and seeing the value in what you do is a great way to do this. It's also a great way to continue cultivating a relationship with yourself. Make sure you're recording every time you have a small or big win so that you can celebrate them all. One of my personal favourites ways to do this is by creating a celebration jar, where you write down your wins on a slip of paper and what you did to celebrate it, then pop it in the jar. You can then open the jar to read them all when you're in need of a little pick-me-up.

# Practical Exercise

Now that we've gone through this time together, we're going to bring it to a close with a ritual to honour all parts of yourself, release what no longer serves you and set some intentions going forward. Let's welcome in the next exciting stage of your journey.

**YOU WILL NEED**

- A pen

- Slips of paper

- Two fireproof bowls

- A lighter or matches

- Water

**TO PERFORM THE RITUAL**

1. Find a relaxing space where you can sit quietly, setting up any candles or relaxing music you think may help. Make sure the space is safe to burn the slips of paper and be sure to have water or a fire extinguisher nearby to safely put any fire out if needed.

2. Become present with where you are now and reflect on everything you have learned about yourself whilst reading this book.

3. Once you feel ready, write down at least three things on the slips of paper that you have recognised no longer serve you, which you plan on releasing or moving away from.

4. Safely burn your slips of paper in the first fireproof bowl, setting the intention to release these things going forward.

5. When you're finished, discard the ashes in the rubbish bin (once they've completely cooled).

6. Next, write down the intentions that you'd like to start bringing in and embracing over the next few months on the slips of paper.

7. Safely burn the slips of paper in the second fireproof bowl, this time with the intention of welcoming these things in.

8. Once the ashes have cooled completely, find a space outside where you can release them into the wind rather than into the bin.

9. When you come back inside, just sit with how you're feeling after the ritual and feel free to journal anything that comes up over the next few hours.

# Some closing words from my heart to yours...

I hope that this book has given you the tools you need to give yourself what you deserve and recognise your value in this world. I hope that you start to see how your authenticity is your true magic, and continue sharing that magic with others. When you feel like your time is over with this book, and you're ready to move on, gift it to someone in your life who needs it.

Keep shining your light.

Love,

Polly

# About the Author

Polly Pollock is a mentor for women on the path of self-rediscovery. She specialises in helping entrepreneurs, creatives and soul-led women step into leadership in their lives and work, by moving through the fear of being seen authentically and shamelessly expressing their unique magic and medicine to the world.

As well as being an author, Polly also works with people through one-to-one coaching, group mentoring, live talks, workshops, retreats and more. To find out more about Polly's work, head over to **www.pollypollock.com.**

# Acknowledgments

Thank you to my other half, Jacque, for helping me realise that my dream of being an author was possible, and for always cheering me on to reach my next goal.

Thank you to my wonderful family – my Dad, Steve, my Mum, Liesl and my brother, Jamie, for your support, love and encouragement, always.

Thank you to my best friend, Claire. Without you, I don't know where I would be with my work today – you are my biggest inspiration.

Thank you to the David & Charles team for making my first book a reality!

Lastly, thank you to all of the brave women before me who paved the way for me to do the work that I do today.

# Index